Web Production for Writers and Journalists

'. . . an excellent insight into the main issues of creating a website and offering a good foundation of knowledge.' *.net magazine*

Web Production for Writers and Journalists is a clear and practical guide to the planning, setting up and management of a web site. It gives readers an overview of the current technologies available for online communications and shows how to use them for maximum effect when planning a web site.

Web Production for Writers and Journalists sets out the practical toolkit needed for web design, from web and image editors to information processing and program applications. Supported by a regularly updated and comprehensive website at **www.producing.routledge.com**, *Web Production for Writers and Journalists* includes:

- Illustrated examples of good page design and site content
- Online support and information on new technologies
- Advice on content, maintenance and how to use sites effectively
- Ideas on how to maximise available programs and applications
- A glossary and a list of Internet terminology

This revised and updated edition includes:

- A comprehensive section on how ethics and Internet regulation affect writers and journalists
- Tutorials for the main applications used in web site design
- Guides to good practice for all those involved in journalism, broadcasting and media studies
- A list of resources including web sites and guides to further reading

Jason Whittaker is a lecturer at Falmouth College of Arts where he teaches courses on digital media and online journalism. He is the author of *The Internet: The Basics*, also published by Routledge, and was previously the editor of *PC Advisor*.

Media Skills

SERIES EDITOR: RICHARD KEEBLE, CITY UNIVERSITY, LONDON
SERIES ADVISERS: WYNFORD HICKS AND JENNY McKAY

The *Media Skills* series provides a concise and thorough introduction to a rapidly changing media landscape. Each book is written by media and journalism lecturers or experienced professionals and is a key resource for a particular industry. Offering helpful advice and information and using practical examples from print, broadcast and digital media, as well as discussing ethical and regulatory issues, *Media Skills* books are essential guides for students and media professionals.

Also in this series:

Find more details of current *Media Skills* books and forthcoming titles at **www.producing.routledge.com**

Web Production for Writers and Journalists

Second edition

www.producing.routledge.com

Jason Whittaker

London and New York

First published 2000 as *Producing for the Web*
by Routledge
11 New Fetter Lane, London EC4P 4EE

Simultaneously published in the USA and Canada
by Routledge
29 West 35th Street, New York, NY 10001

Second edition published 2002

Routledge is an imprint of the Taylor & Francis Group

© 2000, 2002 Jason Whittaker

Typeset in Goudy Oldstyle by
Florence Production Limited, Stoodleigh, Devon
Printed and bound in Great Britain by
TJ International Ltd, Padstow, Cornwall

British Library Cataloguing in Publication Data
A catalogue record for this book is available from the British Library

Library of Congress Cataloging in Publication Data
has been applied for

ISBN 0–415–27251–3 (hbk)
ISBN 0–415–27252–1 (pbk)

Contents

Illustrations

Tables

Figures

Acknowledgements

I would like to thank my colleagues – fellow lecturers, students and especially the staff at *PC Advisor* – for support, comments and suggestions, as well as Christopher Cudmore at Routledge. Particular thanks are due to Sam, for permission to use her photographs, as well as to Adobe and Macromedia for providing software and useful information.

Introduction

What this book is

This book is about producing web sites and using one of the most important parts of the **Internet**, the World Wide Web, to maximum effect. The Web, which was established in the early 1990s and emerged as a mass medium in the second half of that decade, has attracted a huge amount of attention from the more traditional media as well as academic, business and, of course, computer-using communities.

The Web holds out the promise of publishing and communication on a potentially global scale to anyone with access to a computer and online connection. Producing a web site can be pleasurable in itself, developing technical, writing and design skills that culminate in well-crafted pages. When computers work well (and they do not, it must be admitted, always work well), they enable people to develop ideas and achieve things that previously could only be done by experts.

At the same time, these skills – writing about interests and passions, creating graphics and laying out pages, programming scripts and interactive elements – are becoming more important than ever at the start of a new century. Web production and management is becoming a career for more and more people rather than a hobby. As such, web producers need to understand the principles of how sites can work effectively and what abilities they need to develop for this new medium, both on a technical level and to communicate proficiently.

This book is a practical guide for anyone interested in the principles of web production, whether students, professionals or those who may be interested in developing their design skills for personal interests. Creating web sites is no longer the preserve of computer engineers, programmers and scientists but is open to a much wider group.

Part of the reason for the massive explosion of the Web is that designing sites and taking part in this expanding, sprawling, often chaotic medium is that it can be incredible fun. As such, although this book is aimed at professionals seeking to enhance their skills into web production, it should also be read by those with a desire to expand their imagination into a new sphere.

What this book is not

Although this book contains instructions for creating web sites, it is not a manual for particular applications. Most of the books published for use with the Internet and computers are generally aimed at learning a particular program or set of programming techniques. The aim of this book is different. The guides that are provided in the following chapters and the accompanying web site are designed to be transferable across a number of applications, but are also provided as a basis of thinking why such skills are necessary and how they are best used.

Nor is this a book about the Web and the Internet. Although some background is given as to where the Web has come from and why it is important, the main aim of such information is to provide a practical context for producing sites. You will not find instructions on using the Internet or computers in this book. The assumption is that you will already have some familiarity with using a browser and an operating system to save and open files.

This book does not offer reviews of web sites nor purport to be a guide to finding the best sites for particular tasks on the Internet. Examples of good practice and useful web addresses are included, particularly when they illustrate a certain technique or style, but a book of this type cannot, and should not, claim to be a comprehensive listing of an ever-changing medium.

By using this book, you will gain a grounding in the technologies and practical skills that are necessary to create a web site as well as an understanding of ways to plan and promote it to reach as many people as possible.

Why producers?

There are several terms used to describe workers involved in web site production. Some of these are familiar from other media. There are, for example, writers and journalists who generate copy for a web site in the same fashion as staff writers for newspapers and magazines, as well as editors organising content, establishing production calendars and commissioning writers.

Other people may have links to other media but with slight differences. Web designers, for example, may share similarities with art directors and production staff on a magazine, while content-providers creating animation, audio and video for a site may possess some of the same skills as broadcasters for television and radio. In such cases, specialist knowledge of an application such as Quark XPress or Avid may be replaced by Dreamweaver or Flash, but with the convergence of digital technology in more traditional forms of publishing and broadcasting there is considerable scope for crossover.

Finally, there are roles that appear to be more specific to the Web, most notably that of web master which tends to cover technical and managerial skills. The role of web manager often refers to those members of a team who are responsible for meeting deadlines, allocating resources, managing staff and making strategic decisions about the content of a site, similar to the roles of editors, publishers, producers and directors in other media. In other cases, the web manager will also be responsible for the maintenance of a site, writing scripts, ensuring security and installing software, similar to a sound or video engineer; in other organisations these roles are devolved to a separate IT department.

This book uses the term 'producers' to cover all of the above roles. There is, of course, the danger of confusion: if you are interested in web design to advance your career, for example, it is important to be aware that some companies and organisations will be looking for individuals to fulfil very specific roles. Nonetheless, as in other media, web producers are frequently called upon to be multi-tasking. Just as a radio broadcaster may be his or her own sound technician, producer and editor, so web professionals may be called upon to provide different services at different times.

Finally, if you are looking to create a site for personal pleasure, there is a sense in which you are a writer, artist, editor, manager and publisher rolled into one, responsible not just for generating content but also for its distribution and maintenance. While one of the aims of this book is to enable students and professionals to specialise in their chosen field, the ability to direct and shape your own work to an almost unprecedented degree can be incredibly liberating. As one famous multimedia self-publisher, William Blake, remarked, 'I must Create a System, or be enslav'd by another Mans'.

How to use this book

Obviously this book can be read by beginning at the beginning and continuing until you reach the end. Indeed, the chapters are arranged cumulatively, building on concepts, techniques and procedures introduced in previous sections. At the same time, the book is roughly divided into two halves: the first deals with important preparation work that is required to make a web site a success, while the second half deals much more with the mechanics of producing such a site.

In addition, chapters have been organised so that each section may serve as a reference or introduction to a particular aspect of web production. You may, for example, be looking for a particular image or web editor, want to know the difference between Java and ActiveX, or need to understand how to code a rollover button. Thus the book has been designed to also encourage readers to browse as required.

One of the problems with writing about the Web (or, indeed, any aspect of computers) is that there is a huge quantity of technical terms. While much of this is jargon, some of it apparently employed for no other reason than to confuse the novice, much is also precise and to attempt to describe it in 'plain English' can result in sentences that are extremely convoluted. For example, HTML, one of the more common terms, is a useful acronym once the principles of HyperText Markup Language have been explained. I have tried to avoid using technical language simply for its own sake, but where a technical term is first introduced it is highlighted in bold.

Likewise, there are plenty of 'recipes' in the book for creating web pages that require the reader to enter very specific information. When the text indicates that you must type in the text as it appears on the page, a mono-spaced font is used, such as `<title>Hello World</title>`. The reason for this convention is that using quotation marks can be confusing: such punctuation marks are frequently employed in programming code for a specific purpose. Another convention is that web addresses are written without the prefix http:// (which is inserted by most modern browsers in any case). Thus, for example, the address for the popular search engine Google is denoted www.google.com.

Because the Web is such a rapidly evolving medium, there may be some discrepancies between certain sites and what is printed in each chapter. I have attempted to use sites that seem to be the most stable as examples of different techniques and approaches, but sometimes the most interesting work is that produced by individuals who may not be able to sustain a site. Likewise, while writing this book various web editors and applications were updated and re-issued. The book deals with the most up to date information at the time of publication, but it is also designed to be used with the companion web site at www.producing.routledge.com: this site contains updates about software and news that will be of interest to web producers (see the *Web Production for Writers and Journalists* site below).

What you need

The most obvious requirement to use this book is access to a computer and an Internet connection. While you do not actually need to upload files to a site, the latter is useful both for downloading files from the Web and accessing sites that will be useful for web production.

Web design can be incredibly simple in terms of computing power. At a time when computers double in power every eighteen months or so, the Web is often limited by the much slower bottleneck caused by the connection to the Internet. As such, some of the best web design follows the principle that less is more, and it is possible to construct many sites with little more than a text editor such as NotePad on the PC or SimpleText on the Mac.

That said, it is realistic to use a computer that has enough power to run a decent editor and a graphics application to edit images at the very least. This does not need to be the latest Intel or Motorola chip – an older Pentium or Mac will often be more than sufficient for web design, which should *not* consist of manipulating large files.

No assumption has been made about your knowledge of web production, and this book begins with the most basic aspects of web design before proceeding to more complex features. However, there are some things that this book does not cover. It is assumed, for example, that you are familiar with the operating system on the computer you use, that you can open and save files and know how to navigate through the folders on your hard disk. Likewise, this book does not include instructions on how to use browsers to find sites or how to connect to an ISP. It is assumed that you are an Internet user who wishes to move to the next stage and produce your own sites.

The *Web Production for Writers and Journalists* site

Because of the nature of this particular book, the companion web site at www.producing.routledge.com/default.htm is extremely important. You can use this book without referring to the site (for example, using your own images and texts instead of those downloaded from the site), but the site is an expansion of this book.

Although the site does not contain information on issues around planning and maintenance that are important to someone seeking a professional career in web production, it does expand on the tutorials given in this book for different applications and technologies. In addition, information about the Web and

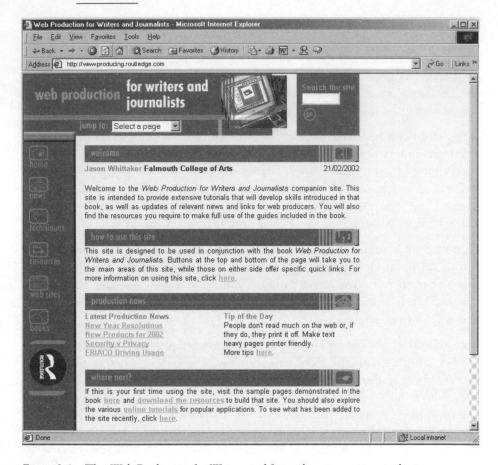

Figure 0.1   The *Web Production for Writers and Journalists* companion web site

web production can change very rapidly, and so the site includes updates about the latest developments.

The site is arranged into the following main areas:

- **Production news**   This includes the latest information relevant to web producers, such as updates to browsers and software, new releases and changes to Internet specifications. The news can be accessed at www. producing.routledge.com/news.htm.

- **Production techniques**   These are extended tutorials for specific packages rather than introductions to principles of web design as in the book. It is assumed that you will have read Chapters 4 and 5 in particular to understand why these techniques are used before accessing the tutorials at www.producing.routledge.com/techniques.htm to see how they are implemented by different programs.

- **Production resources** There is an extended and annotated list of resources listed before the index in this book, as well as files to create the sample site outlined in this book at www.producing.routledge.com/resources.htm.

- **Sample site** Chapters 4 and 5 outline different web production processes with reference to a sample site that you will build using the resources accessed at the above address. To view the sample site, go to www.producing.routledge.com/kernow/default.htm.

1
Worldwide information and communication

The reasons for producing a web site are numerous: it may be part of a project assignment for a university or college course or to market a business; you might have a personal interest that you wish to publish to a wider audience, or you might need to set up a site to promote the activities of a group to which you belong. Whatever the reason for creating a web site, whether as part of a programme of study or development of career skills, web production and publishing is attracting a great deal of attention from employers, the media and the general public as an exciting and important new venture. What was, less than a decade ago, the preserve of enthusiasts has become a mass medium to compare with television, radio and print. It may be affected by fluctuations and downturns, bust as well as boom, but the Internet is here to stay.

This chapter will introduce the background of the Internet, what it is and how it works. As the aim of this book is to provide advice for those seeking to develop their practical skills, some of the theoretical concerns around the Internet such as its history have been kept fairly short. It is not a technical introduction, though it will also introduce some of the jargon associated with the Internet and Web: it is possible to create a web site with a minimum of technical knowledge as to how the Internet actually operates. Nonetheless, some technical knowledge (such as why hosts are required to serve pages) can improve your skills as a web producer. Another aim of this chapter is to consider some of the major players on the Web, their Net strategy and how they intend to move forward in this new medium.

The Internet and the Web

What is the Internet?

The Internet is attracting more and more attention as the next step for worldwide computing. The term, Internet, refers to the connection of millions of computers and users – by 1999 there were 56 million hosts worldwide according to the International Telecommunications Union, and, according to the survey company NUA (www.nua.ie), the best 'educated guess' placed the number of users at around 513 million by August 2001.

The common starting point for any definition of the Internet is as a 'network of networks'. The Internet is a Wide Area Network (WAN), millions of PCs, Apple Macs, mainframes, laptops and other computers joined by cables, satellites and radio waves across the globe. When most people think of the Internet, the first thing that springs into their minds is the hardware, the physical links connecting these diverse parts. Actually, the Internet is equally a collection of communication protocols, rules governing the transfer of information such as TCP/IP (Transfer Control Protocol/Internet Protocol) that allows very different types of computers to communicate with each other. It is this series of protocols, outlasting advances in hardware, which is the lifeblood of the Net.

People tend to think of the Web and the Internet as the same entity. In fact, the Web developed in the 1990s as a means of exchanging documents that piggy-backed across the infrastructure of hardware and software that had developed by that time. The Internet is the larger collection of network services (including email and file transfer), most of which have been integrated into web browsers.

A brief history of the Internet

The beginning of the Internet is conventionally dated to the late 1960s, though one convenient starting point is the launch of Sputnik in 1957, the first artificial satellite that began the space race and the global telecommunications system that the Internet would plug into.

Following the launch of Sputnik, the Advanced Research Projects Agency (ARPA) was founded, essentially funded by the US Department of Defense but also oriented towards academic research. As John Naughton points out in his book, A Brief History of the Future (1999), the actual development of the network of networks we use today owed more to simple academic and financial concerns of using computers more efficiently by networking them together, but the cold war remained an important impetus to the development of ARPA.

Between 1963 and 1967, ARPA investigated the feasibility of building such a network and selected nineteen participants to join in **ARPANET**, as it had become known, work beginning in 1968. Much of the essential work at ARPA consisted of providing the protocols that would enable the physical backbone to communicate. Of especial importance was **packet** switching software: rather than sending information as a single file, it is split into small packets, each of which can be sent via different hosts so that significant amounts of the file reach its destination even in the event of a particular host being unavailable.

International connections were established in 1973 with the University College of London and the Royal Radar Establishment in Norway. Work also proceeded on improving the protocols that remain the standard for Internet transmissions such as file transfer protocol (**FTP**) and transfer control protocol (**TCP**). In 1979, the US National Science Foundation (**NSF**) established a computer science research network.

More significant development began in the 1980s, and it is hardly a coincidence that the largest computer network in the world began to take off as the personal computer gained ground, introducing more and more people to the notion of computing. The 1980s also saw the introduction of Domain Name Services (**DNS**), to allocate addresses to host computers. Throughout the late 1980s, with DNS in place, all these different networks could access computers anywhere across the network, meaning that the Internet was fully established by 1990, the year when ARPANET, its work finished, ceased to exist. The next decade was to establish the Internet as a wider communication medium with the spread of email and development of the Web.

At the European Centre for Nuclear Research (CERN), a consultant, Tim Berners-Lee, had written a short program modestly entitled 'Enquire-Within-Upon-Everything', which enabled electronic documents to be linked more easily. ENQUIRE, as it came to be known, was Berners-Lee's big idea: it became even bigger in 1989, when he submitted a paper entitled 'Information Management: A Proposal'. In 1990, the first text web browser, NeXT, was developed at CERN and so the World Wide Web was born.

CERN continued to develop the Web as an academic tool, but by the end of 1992 only 26 hosts were serving web sites, and even in early 1994 there were only 1,500 registered web servers. The boom in Web – and Internet – growth shown in Figure 1.1 came with the development of Mosaic, a graphical browser

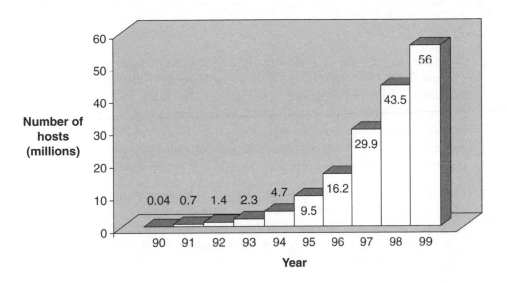

Figure 1.1 Internet hosts worldwide

capable of displaying images as well as text, by Marc Andreessen at the National Center for Supercomputing Applications.

In 1994, Andreessen left to form Mosaic Communications, the precursor to Netscape. What was most significant about Andreessen's work was that he actively began to promote the Internet as a platform, like **UNIX**, or Windows. Nineteen ninety-five was the year of the Web: Netscape Navigator had an estimated 10 million users worldwide and, when the company went public, Netscape Communications was valued at over $2.5 billion on Wall Street.

By this time, Microsoft had 80 per cent of the operating system market, making founder Bill Gates the richest man in the world. Microsoft initially dismissed the Internet as a fad, intending to supplant it with its own Microsoft Network (MSN), but by late 1995 Gates had turned the company around when it was clear that MSN would do no such thing. That the most powerful software company in the world should wish to stake the future of its success on the Web is an indication of just how important it had become – so much so that the Department of Justice (DOJ) launched its biggest investigation of the company in 1997, looking into allegations of abuse of a monopolistic position regarding the bundling of Internet Explorer with the Windows operating system. Although the browser was given away for free, a rash of public offerings had apparently made millionaires – even billionaires – of founders of dotcoms such as Jeff Bezos, the CEO of Amazon.com.

Better by design

Over the past couple of years, the Web has generated its own form of Oscars, the Webby Awards, or 'Webbies', presented by the International Academy of Digital Arts and Sciences to innovative and exceptional sites across a wide range of categories (www.webbyawards.com). The fifth annual awards were held in July 2001 and, as with the four previous ceremonies, two prizes were presented in each category, one for 'official' nominees, the other for popular choices voted for by Internet users.

Despite the bad news that had dogged technology companies during 2000 and 2001, the hosts of the Webbies still managed to place a positive spin on participants they described as 'the risk takers, the innovators, the believers' – even though there were considerably fewer of all three than two years previously.

There are thirty categories, including a special award for Best Practice, and some of my favourite sites include: Young-Hae Chang Heavy

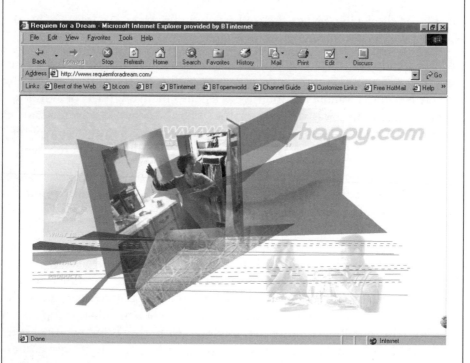

Figure 1.2 Requiem for a Dream – one of the Webby-winning sites that indicate obituaries for the Web are premature

Industries (www.yhchang.com), a minimalist Flash site that demonstrates in seconds why less is often more; NationalGeographic.com (www.nationalgeographic.com), one of the best 'old media' titles to make the transition to the Web; the site for the film *Requiem for a Dream* (www.requiemforadream.com), itself a work of art to match a great movie; Sputnik 7 (www.sputnik7.com), a video and music site that reminds jaded users with broadband access that there was a time when 'cool site of the day' made sense; and Google (www.google.com), which deservedly won the award for Best Practice. While many other award-winning sites are experimental and innovative, Google is the fastest, most efficient and easiest to use search engine around.

Over the next four years, Microsoft suffered public humiliation after public humiliation, and it even appeared at one point that the company would be broken up. Microsoft escaped this fate in February 2001, when the federal appeals court reversed some of the DOJ's findings and criticised District Judge Thomas Penfield Jackson. Nonetheless, while the appeals court maintained that aggressively marketing Internet Explorer did not violate the Sherman Act, the judges also argued that Microsoft's Windows-only agreements with PC manufacturers did mean that the company had behaved anti-competitively and that it should be held liable for its actions.

At the same time that companies such as Sun, AOL and Microsoft were fighting over the future of the Internet market, the prize they sought seemed to go into meltdown as web companies disappeared or became almost worthless. Startups such as Boo.com failed dramatically in the middle of 2000, while those that did not immediately collapse, such as QXL or LastMinute.com, had the dubious honour of joining the 99 per cent club – where stocks fell by 99 per cent following flotation, or collapsed before such a flotation could take place as in the case of Jungle. The immediate consequences of the recession have been disastrous for new technologies: yet the simple truth is that the boom at the end of the 1990s could never be sustained. In the mid- to long-term, investment in the Internet is likely to be less spectacular but more stable, with analysts such as PricewaterhouseCoopers reporting in *Money for Growth* (2001) that venture capitalists remained positive about investments in technology, while avoiding weak areas such as WAP and inexperienced dotcoms.

How the Internet works

The basic architecture of the Internet is what is known as a **client-server** model. A server, a computer running special software, hosts a range of services such as email and web pages which are accessed by client software running on a remote computer. Most users access servers via a dial-up account with an **ISP** and it is worth knowing some basic details about how ISPs connect their users to the Net.

An Internet Service Provider (ISP) is a company or organisation that provides dial-up accounts by purchasing a leased line connection and then dividing its use between subscribers. There are hundreds in the UK and thousands worldwide. Dial-up ISPs offer Point-to-Point Protocol (**PPP**) or Serial Line Internet Protocol (**SLIP**) accounts to users, the superior PPP accounts being most common.

PPP communications programs, such as Windows Dial-Up Networking, connect to the network by dialling via a **modem**, then log into the network with a user name and password. Windows application producers created a standard way for Internet clients to communicate called Winsock (short for Windows sockets, the protocols governing the ports listed under 'Servers, Clients and Ports' below) and Dial-Up Networking is Winsock compatible. The equivalent standard for Macs is called Open Transport/PPP in earlier versions of the MacOS, Apple Remote Access in the latest version.

Internet structure

The Internet backbone is comprised of two main parts: the hardware/communications network, and the protocols governing data transfer across that network. The actual computer hardware is relatively insignificant, in that it can be upgraded regularly and is changed frequently. More important is the communications infrastructure, the cables and satellite links, which are much more difficult to change and limit the **bandwidth**, the amount of data, that can be transferred from computer to computer. A common metaphor for bandwidth is a pipe, but this is incredibly misleading: the assumption is that if you increase the width of the pipe, you can pour more data down it. A better metaphor is of a road network: simply widening roads may not help traffic jams, but smaller and faster cars, as well as improved traffic control systems, might help more drivers get from A to B.

Protocols control how data is transferred across that infrastructure, the most important ones being collected together as TCP/IP (transfer control protocol/

Internet protocol). TCP/IP operates on four levels: network access (to facilitate transmission and routeing of packets); network protocols (governing the delivery service); transfer protocols (ensuring the machines are capable of receiving and sending packets); and application protocols (either applications themselves, or providing service to applications running across the Internet).

IP addressing is the basic means by which computers are identified on the Net. This is a 32-bit number that uniquely identifies each host and network as four octets from 0 to 255 (for example, 10.126.58.192). Along with the IP address is a host name, a more easily memorised name (such as www.ibm.com): the Domain Name Service (DNS) is a table holding lists of hosts, so that when a user sends an email, requests are passed up the Internet chain until eventually they find a DNS table listing that host. Information passed from computers is broken into packets, each one with a heading that identifies that packet: when they reach their destination, the packets are reassembled into the complete message. Some of the protocols governing TCP/IP are error-checking protocols: if the message is incomplete, the destination computer requests the packet to be sent again.

Protocols and services

After connecting to the Internet, there are various different protocols and services used to transmit information to the client.

- **Web documents**   The Web is a collection of sites, or documents, which share a specialised protocol, HyperText Transfer Protocol (**HTTP**), enabling different operating systems to share the same data. Web documents are formatted in **HTML**, or HyperText Markup Language, to standardise the presentation of text, graphics and links to other sites, with the end result that a document will look more or less the same in a browser for Windows, MacOS or UNIX. Clicking on a hypertext link, which is an embedded address or **URL**, will effect a transfer of information, whether to another document, image or file. **Hypertext** is something of a misnomer, as links within a web document can also be anchored to images.

- **HTTP**   HyperText Transfer Protocol enables the easy retrieval of documents from the Internet regardless of where they are held. HTTP defines URLs not only for the Web but also FTP, Gopher and Usenet sites, making it an extremely useful means of accessing a wide range of documents. To implement data transfer as simply as possible, HTTP provides web authors with the ability to embed hypertext links within documents.

- **URL**   A Uniform Resource Locator (usually signified as http://) is an address identifying an Internet document's type and location. URLs are absolute or relative, the former indicating precisely where a document is to be found on the Web, the latter assuming that the file is a document somewhere on the same site.

- **FTP**   As a network of networks, the Internet is a large repository of software and information. Before the Web boom, an older method of accessing this data was via the extremely useful method of FTP (File Transfer Protocol), which has subsequently been absorbed into many browsers. FTP was developed to enable users to run client programs and access remote archives managed by FTP servers. Using a web browser FTP sites are accessed by following links, while FTP client software requires users to log onto a site.

- **Usenet**   Usenet consists of several thousand newsgroups on a vast number of topics, newsgroups being identified by prefixes such as rec. (recreational) or alt. (alternative). Accessing Usenet enables users to read articles or post replies for other subscribers and most web browsers are capable of reading Usenet news. There are few or no formal rules governing Usenet forums (but plenty of informal ones), and this can make Usenet overwhelming at first. If you have a special interest, however, a newsgroup may be a cheap and convenient means of retrieving information.

- **IRC**   Internet Relay Chat is the Internet's real-time facility, enabling users to log onto the Net at the same time and carry on sentence-by-sentence conversations. IRC runs via channels, discussion areas which exist in their thousands; you can send messages to everyone on such a channel, or to individuals.

- **Telnet**   Telnet is a protocol allowing users to log into a remote computer and use it as their own. The most common uses for Telnet are logging into a computer to pick up email or to use specific programs. When a PC is connected to a remote computer, it acts very much like a terminal, with Telnet protocol emulating terminal standards that used to govern connections to large mainframes.

Servers, clients and ports

While many Internet users can use the Web with minimum knowledge of how its computers are connected as a network, web producers, especially those responsible for managing sites, may find a basic understanding helpful, particularly when loading sites onto remote computers. The above protocols and services require the following servers:

- **Mail servers** Handling incoming and outgoing mail, Post Office Protocol (**POP**, or POP3) servers store incoming mail and Simple Mail Transfer Protocol (**SMTP**) servers send outgoing mail.

- **Web servers** These hold web pages that are downloaded to client browsers.

- **FTP servers** Store files that can be transferred (via the File Transfer Protocol) to and from a computer with a suitable client.

- **News servers** News servers hold text messages – Usenet newsgroup articles – which are a popular forum for discussion on the Internet.

- **IRC servers** These are switchboards for Internet Relay Chat, real-time based communication online.

A single computer can host more than one server, so that small ISPs will tend to have one computer running a mail server, web server and newsgroup server. To handle requests from different clients, each server type responds to information sent to a specific **port**, the input for that specific Internet service. Port numbers are increasingly handled by client software, but occasionally it may be necessary to specify the port when connecting to an ISP for the first time, for example to upload files via FTP onto a remote server (see Table 1.1).

For example, in some cases connecting to an FTP server would require you to enter the address followed by a colon and port number ftp://ftp.myaddress.com:21.

Table 1.1   Server ports

Port number	Service
21	FTP
23	Telnet
25	SMTP
80	Web
110	POP3

King content

An old adage states that 'content is king': there is more than a little wishful thinking to this saying – great content did not, for example, prevent sites such as *Suck* or *Feed* from disappearing.

Nonetheless, the reason why Internet users return again and again to the Web as opposed to email or chat rooms, where participation is all, is due to the material they find online. Much of this may be of dubious quality or even illegal, such as pornography or pirated MP3 files, but many sites are reporting increased traffic even as the medium as a whole is supposedly stagnating.

For many of the largest and best web sites, it is clear that they form part of a strategy to gain maximum leverage from content that may be produced elsewhere in an institution. BBC.co.uk, CNN.com and guardianunlimited.co.uk, for example, have geared up their online activities to provide a comprehensive service. Nor does this, in the best

Figure 1.3   Old media meets new – the GuardianUnlimited web site

cases, detract from 'old media': The *Guardian*, for example, has reported year-on-year rises in sales for its newspaper.

While the promises of broadband have been slow in coming, sites such as Heavy (a 2001 Webby winner, www.heavy.com) and Jolt TV (www.jolttv.com) are presenting themselves as alternatives to conventional forms of entertainment. Their time has not arrived yet, and when all Internet users have fast **ADSL** or cable connections many of these early innovators will have disappeared. Nonetheless, they indicate the potential of the future Web.

Finally, one site with simply brilliant content indicates almost single-handedly why the Web exists. *The Onion* (www.theonion.com), winner of the comedy web award for the second year in a row, was initially a small circulation newspaper from nowheresville, America. Now millions of visitors each year enjoy headlines such as 'Stunned Nation Mourns As French Stewart Survives Plane Crash' and 'Don't Run Away, I'm Not The Flesh-Eating Kind of Zombie', people who would otherwise never have the chance to enjoy the eccentric humour of *The Onion*'s editors.

Browsers

Browsers are, strictly speaking, programs designed to communicate with web servers on the Internet, but common usage extends the term for the two most popular browsers, Netscape (formerly known as Navigator or Communicator) and Microsoft Internet Explorer, to cover email, newsgroup and other functions. These browsers also use **plug-ins**, applications loaded by the browser to extend its functionality, to perform certain tasks such as playing certain audio-visual files or displaying some 3D sites.

A web browser utilises HTTP to communicate with a server and then translates HTML code to display pages on the client computer. At its absolute minimum, this means a browser must display text, but since the incorporation of images, users have come to expect much more, and the latest versions of Navigator and Internet Explorer (IE) can display video, sound, 3D and interactive animation. The versatility of browsers has made them increasingly important outside the Web, so that from IE 4 and Windows 98 onwards, Microsoft has begun to build its browser into the operating system to display files and images.

Competition between Netscape and Microsoft is fierce, and was a main contributor to the anti-trust case against Microsoft in 1997. While this has had many negative effects, principally issues around compatibility, it has also helped to fuel development of web technologies as computing power has increased since the early 1990s. Both companies tend to update their browsers on a regular basis (currently up to version 6 for Netscape and IE) and latest versions are available from their web sites:

home.netscape.com/computing/download/index.html

www.microsoft.com/windows/ie/default.htm

These are not the only browsers available on the Web: Opera (www.opera-software.com) is a recent newcomer and there may even be a very few visitors with older machines still using Mosaic, the first graphical browser, and Lynx, a text-only browser, although this is highly unlikely. Most browsers have the same basic layout – a menu bar, toolbars (with back, forward, reload and other buttons located here), an address or location window, the main viewing window where pages are displayed, and a status bar indicating such things as download time.

The web market

Boom or bust?

The market for web production has changed significantly since this book was first published in 2000. At that time, motivated in part by the need for many companies to replace old technology in the face of a potential millennium bug, as well as a rush to be part of the 'next big thing', many venture capitalists and ordinary investors created an extremely buoyant market for dotcom companies. For a brief period of time it appeared that all one needed to become a millionaire was a good idea and a web site – and even the good idea was optional.

As we have already seen, the dotcom boom of 1999–2000 has largely gone the way of tulipomania or the South Sea Bubble: many companies were clearly inflated in terms of their stock market value at the time of launch and were also run by inexperienced staff. The notion that the so-called 'New Economy' could operate according to original rules (where concepts such as generating revenue did not matter) was obviously false for the media industry. In particular, the reliance of many producers on advertising left them vulnerable to the subsequent recession that began to bite at the end of 2000.

And yet, Internet usage is on the increase: despite the fact that many users enjoy a 'honeymoon' period when they surf the Web enthusiastically and then fall into more sedentary habits, the number of homes where Internet access is available climbs steadily each year. The Napster phenomenon (discussed in Chapter 6) also indicates some of the ways in which the Net is also genuinely revolutionising the media: by failing to deal adequately with issues around copyright Napster was doomed to fail, yet many users also indicated that they would be willing to pay for music online – although not necessarily on the terms set by the major record labels alone.

The Web is still an immature medium and, in part, has been the victim of its own early success. The rapid rise of sites at the end of the 1990s was motivated by a greedy, get-rich-quick mentality as companies raced to become the next Microsoft (without its regulatory difficulties). Despite the spectacular crashes of many businesses that failed to get it right, there have also been some sites that have succeeded very well. As Owen Gibson (2001) remarks: 'Just as it was folly to take seriously the vast unsustainable investments promised in digital projects during the Web's salad days, so there is a danger of swinging too far the other way.'

Sites that survive and flourish

The web market has contracted, then, in the early twenty-first century, but this is a necessary corrective to the madness that operated at the end of the twentieth. What remains will be more solid, more sustainable. Throughout this book, you will be guided through the practicalities of creating a successful web site from the planning to marketing stages, but the following indicate some why a few of the sites considered in this chapter thrive on the Web.

- **Merge and consolidate**   Only a few years ago, the movement in the media industries towards greater centralisation seemed to be precisely the trend that the Internet would buck. Small, nimble companies and sites would be able to respond to markets more quickly than lumbering dinosaurs such as AOL. In 2001, the successful merger of AOL with Time Warner has made this particular behemoth not only the largest Internet player alongside Microsoft, but also the company best placed to take advantage of the Web in years to come. On a smaller scale, many traditional businesses have bought up dotcoms to pursue a 'clicks and mortar' strategy, combining experienced management with new-technology know-how.

- **Leverage existing content**   One of the main reasons for the AOL–Time Warner merger comes from the fact that AOL needs more and more content for its customers; at the same time it provides Time Warner with the technological knowledge (and large customer base) to transfer such content to the new medium. Time Warner had tried to do this before with its Pathfinder site (www.pathfinder.com), but tended to shovel print content onto the Web in a rather dull fashion. Other sites that have been bold and original in terms of utilising existing material include the BBC.co.uk and The *Guardian* web site, guardianunlimited.co.uk. Not only do these sites draw upon well-recognised content produced to a very high standard, their sites work to leverage that content in a new context, providing bulletin boards, additional background context for stories or programmes, and repurposing material in a fashion that is easier to use on screen (shorter stories, for example).

- **Update content regularly**   This is an obvious condition for a successful web site, but one that has not always been followed, primarily because after a time only the most dedicated web producer will continue to work on a site for nothing: if cash runs out, then so does content. There are a few sites, such as APB Online (a crime web site at www.apbnews.com) and Orato (www.orato.com), which are examples of how not to plan for new content: if they still exist when you try to access them, you'll find them run by volunteers on an irregular basis.

- **Build an audience**   Regular, good-quality content is essential to generating an audience, although this is not quite the touchstone of web success that it was until recently. Having a million visitors a month does not mean that you will be able to ensure your site's survival. In the meantime, however, successful web sites such as Yahoo and *Salon* (www.salon.com) concentrate on building an audience by providing an easy to use web site that allows easy navigation to the information that the visitor requires, as well as plenty of opportunities for involvement and feedback, such as forums and chat rooms. Beware: audiences are fickle. In the magazine trade, this is known as being 'promiscuous', and indicates that most consumers will buy your title one week and a competitor's the next without any feelings of regret. Blaming visitors for this is generally as effective as blaming the free market: work out a strategy to improve your site and get over it.

Regular information on the state of web markets can be found in the News section of *Web Production for Writers and Journalists* site at www.producing. routledge.com/news.htm.

2
Pre-production
Planning and organisation

Nearly a decade ago, the question 'Why make a web site?' had a very simply answer: because it was there. Now it is no longer enough for this medium to be cool simply because it represents new technology, it must also offer core benefits to users. The Internet – and the Web especially – is becoming much more of a practical tool for commerce, entertainment and communication.

With the Web, you can receive constantly changing reports on weather and travel, book tickets, locate and study for courses and receive information, goods and services on everything from upgrading your computer to groceries. Despite setbacks, Internet shopping has finally established itself, with businesses moving beyond using the Web simply for email and teleworking to providing online catalogues and credit services.

To utilise the benefits of the Web requires careful pre-planning: before launching into web production, it is important to think strategically about the potential benefits that a web site may offer, how designers and users will connect to such a site and how projects will be maintained and developed.

First steps

Why a web site?

The first questions to ask when considering the possibilities of a web site are: do you need it, and what can Internet communication achieve that traditional forms cannot?

With regard to the second question, the most obvious factor is the use of the Internet for communication via email and web pages. Like the telephone or fax, the Internet is (usually) fast but, like a letter, can be viewed or responded to at the user's convenience. It may not be as useful as the phone for reaching a quick decision between two people, but, due to the fact that an email can consist of anything from a simple text message to a full-blown multimedia file, it is a more versatile medium than any other.

Turning to whether a web site is necessary for a business or an individual such as a student looking to complete a project, an important consideration is whether the Web will enhance or decrease productivity. The rationale for a web site can be summarised by the following questions:

- **What is it for and who is the intended audience?**   Web sites can be used for many purposes, including sharing an interest, e-commerce, publicising goods and services, product branding, or public information services. Establishing the target audience is important as an indicator for whether the site will meet its aims: creating an information site for people without access to the Web, for example, is not likely to achieve any significant aims.

- **Can you afford a web site?**   As well as the obvious category of hiring web space on a server (which will almost certainly be negligible assuming the site is to be hosted on an ISP) and designing the site in the first place, this covers the cost of time as well as money to produce and maintain a web site. Even for larger companies there is the problem of ensuring sufficient time to update information and deal with the communications that (you hope) will be generated by the site.

- **What are your strategic aims?**   You should decide what you are using the web site for, which could include assessing the demographics of customers, the current market place, or, if you are a student, whether producing a web site will fulfil your aims better than, say, an essay.

- **How will you judge the success of your site?**   This includes setting in place criteria by which you can evaluate whether or not a site achieves your aims. For example, this may consist of basic statistical information such as the number of hits your site generates, or something more substantial, such as diverting phone calls from support lines to a web site or achieving pass grades for a student.

- **How will you promote your site?**   If you are going to use the Web seriously, don't complain if you forget to tell anyone and then receive a lacklustre response. Promotion can be as simple as including a URL on a business card, or as expensive as taking out advertising banners on other sites. One necessity is to register your site with search engines so that casual users will be able to find relevant information.

Internet or intranet?

For the aspiring web producer, probably the most important decision is whether you will be building an internet or **intranet** web site. Both employ many of the same features and technologies (web pages linked to a server, often hosting some form of database) and the skills outlined in this book will, in most cases, apply to either, but the function of an intranet as opposed to an Internet site is often very different.

While an Internet site is built from the start to be accessible to users with browsers on the World Wide Web, intranet sites may be housed entirely within a single geographical location. It is more likely, because they use protocols such as HTTP and FTP to transmit information, that intranets will be a hybrid, accessed by users within a company or at home and on the road, but with greater attention to security.

Although web sites and intranets share the same technologies, the requirements of their users are very different. Simply setting up a web server such as **Apache** or Microsoft **IIS** on a server in a company with some pages and a database does not constitute an intranet. An intranet that is not used by people will be a failure, so whereas a web site may be a success simply because it provides a link between your enthusiasms and the outside world, an intranet must have content that is compelling to its users.

To be fully successful, then, an intranet should invite its users to take ownership of that content. Most of the data within an organisation is not going to be controlled by one person (the web producer), so there should be the possibility of updating information by other people. This raises the spectre of security, particularly if users will access the site across the Internet, so designing an intranet requires additional attention to areas on a server where users will be able to add information and those which are not to be accessed.

The Web and commerce

The end of the 1990s saw a huge boom in Internet production whereby it seemed a new paper millionaire was produced every day. By the middle of 2000, the dotcom bubble had burst and many companies have disappeared or suffered huge cutbacks. Nonetheless, one of the main reasons for interest in developing web sites is still centred on retail, with the Web providing not only new levels of service and support for existing customers but also sales channels for new markets. It can serve as a platform for entirely new ventures, such as Amazon.com, an Internet sales outlet which shook major traditional book-sellers such as Barnes and Noble and WH Smith, causing them to rethink their own online presence.

A key area, for example, where the Internet has been useful for businesses is as a supplement to mail order services (where a database of products already exists in paper format). While creating an HTML catalogue with ordering support is increasingly simple, it may result in some operational difficulties that emphasise the importance of pre-production planning. Reaching a world-wide audience implies a 24-hour service, including customer support.

The full process of planning for an e-commerce site is beyond the remit of this book. Those interested in setting up an e-commerce site that can process orders around the clock will require a payment processor and merchant agreement in order to accept credit card payments, such as those provided by Barclays Merchant Services (www.bms.barclays.co.uk) or NetBanx (www. netbanx.com). Such services typically charge startup fees and a levy on each transaction that takes place.

Once a merchant agreement and payment processor are established, a secure link is set up between the customer and processor service: many ISPs offer support for this, but expect to pay extra. When information is sent to the processor, details are also passed to the customer and merchant that payment has been accepted, then transferred to the online company so that the order can be sent out.

Services with the aim of simplifying online commerce include Yahoo! Store (store.yahoo.com), Free Merchant (www.freemerchant.com), and BigStep (www.bigstep.com). Some of these, as the names imply, are free, but expect to pay a small fee for more secure services.

Planning

Managing the project

Probably one area that is neglected when creating web pages is how to manage it as a project but, if a web site is to be a success, resources must be allocated, deadlines observed and tasks established.

Anyone involved in project management will be presented with a job for which they have limited workers, time and resources. The first step in managing more effectively is to divide a complex project into essential tasks that can be assigned deadlines and be set in order. More than this, however, successful project management requires allocating resources – whether money or workers – as well as providing warnings should these fall behind schedule.

In addition to ensuring that workers and time are allocated to meet a deadline, effective management should consider the consequences on deadlines and work if budgetary constraints are applied, for example how much work can be achieved if a certain amount of money is cut or moved elsewhere, or which tasks will have to be prioritised if deadlines are changed.

To make the process easier, a project can be divided into four distinct sections: defining the project, creating a project plan, tracking the project and then closing it. A project plan that maps out tasks and deadlines can be an indispensable tool for defining clearly the scope and resources available. The first step is to ensure that a realistic scope and deadlines for producing a web site are set, ensuring that assumptions can be met. To help with this, a project plan breaks down the project into tasks that can be assigned different resources and workers, having identified who or what will fulfil each task.

A project plan can proceed by one of two ways: a project start date is entered and the plan is scheduled forward to determine the best deadline, or the completion date is entered and tasks scheduled backwards. Once people and resources are assigned to tasks, the essential building blocks, resources, need to be tracked, both to ensure that work is spread as evenly as possible and also to plan for eventualities such as ill-health or other work.

Closing a project is, typically, the successful delivery of a web site. However, one of the main mistakes made when creating an Internet or intranet site is failing to provide for its running costs, particularly in terms of time for maintenance. As such, closing a particular project may be establishing completion of the first stage, but will look forward to requirements and allocations for updates and managing the site.

Registering a domain name

While a web site may be hosted in a number of locations, determined principally by costs and technical support, one feature that is essential to make a mark on the Web is a registered domain name, the web address that users type into their browser. Domain names are effectively the 'real estate' of the Internet, with easy to remember names being the virtual equivalent of prime site addresses.

Top level domain names (**TLDs**) are registered with a non-profit body, the Internet Corporation for Assigned Names and Numbers (**ICANN**, www. icann.org), which holds a list of accredited registrars. Registration of domain names has become something of a business in its own right, with many entrepreneurial individuals and businesses engaging in a practice known as cybersquatting, buying up names that are likely to be requested and then charging a not-so-modest sum to transfer the name to a new owner. After several recent high-profile court cases, certain companies will no longer allow users to register commercial brand names or trademarks, although some Internet users and regulators are divided over this issue. In addition, the process of registering TLDs has recently become more complex: early in 2001, ICANN announced a number of new TLDs such as .info and .pro but New.net, an American company, has also offered up to 30 TLDs including .club, .shop and .xxx, many of which were turned down by ICANN.

Tips for registering a domain name

- While certain key addresses (in particular bbc.co.uk) have made the .co.uk suffix popular in the UK, if your site is in any way international a .com address is advisable.

- If the domain name is part of a registered trademark or you want to prevent competitors using similar names to attract business, register as many variants (.com, .co.uk, .net) as possible. Also remember that ICANN has recently announced a raft of new TLDs such as .info and .pro.

- Domain names ending in the suffix .com are restricted to 22 or fewer characters. Those ending in .co.uk can have up to 80 characters.

- Letters, numbers and hyphens can form part of a domain name, but not other characters or spaces.

- At the time of writing, the direct registration fee is approximately £80 over two years for a .com address and typically much less (as low as £5 or even free) for a .co.uk address, although this only applies to Nominet members who are charged £5 per domain name. These fees have to be renewed every two years, and extra costs may be incurred for services such as redirecting email and hosting your web site.

These new TLDs actually exist under the New.net address so that www. sports.club is seen by ICANN as www.sports.club.new.net. For the addresses to be viewable as widely as possible, ISPs will need to download a redirection utility from New.net: it is estimated that about 50 million users can currently view these new domain names, a number that New.net hoped to double by the end of 2001. With the increasing commercialisation of the Internet, this is one more example that the 'gentlemen's agreement' between academic and government organisations that once dictated the shape of the Web will come under greater pressure.

Many of the most obvious and best addresses (such as www.clickhere.com) have already been registered, as have phrases (www.coolsiteoftheday.com), but you can check whether a domain name is still available for registration at Nominet (www.nic.uk). You may even wish to reserve a domain name for which you do not yet have a web presence. By 2001, 25 million .com, .net and .org names had been registered – not all are active, however, and you can check to see whether a domain name has expired (and can thus be re-registered) at www. redhotdomainnames.com.

If the particular name you desire has already been snapped up, be inventive and consider possible variants of your name or the nature of your enterprise. When you find a combination that is still available, there are a few rules and tips that apply to registering a domain name (see p. 29).

Planning the workflow

Before even beginning planning that will determine the structure and content of a web site, the first step is to determine a process model by which work will develop. Rather than including pages and content on an ad-hoc basis, a simple development model is often referred to as a 'waterfall model' whereby the function of the web site is defined, a prototype is built and tested before the final site is released, with feedback occurring at each stage as in Figure 2.1.

Regarding the initial stage of this process model, it is important to define the function of the site, its purpose and audience. This can create problems for web developers in that they are not the final users: it is important to get feedback from users, but it is advisable (and this comes from personal experience) to negotiate a limit to such feedback from the beginning. Once a web site begins to roll out it is very easy to be caught in a wish-list that quickly muddies the parameters of what a site should accomplish, with the final result that such a site ends up pleasing nobody any of the time in its attempt to fulfil everyone's requirements all of the time.

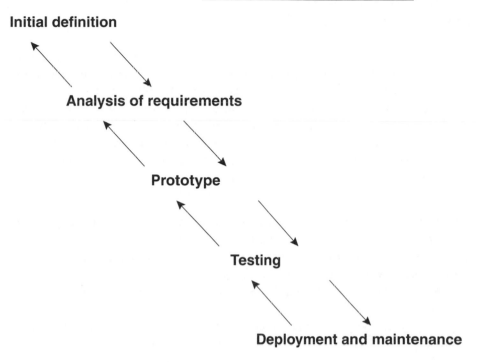

Figure 2.1 The 'waterfall model'

Much has been said about 'user-centred design', but there are issues around targeting the average user – particularly whether such a figure actually exists. That said, there probably are some fundamentals that affect nearly all web production. First of all, speed is key: most users expect pages to load almost instantly (though this is less of an issue across an intranet or broadband connection than it is across a dial-up modem); as a rule of thumb, any page that takes more than ten seconds to download will lose visitors. Secondly, because the end-user's browser cannot always be guaranteed, it is important to test a site's appearance in multiple browsers. Finally, a site's audience does not wish to appreciate its appearance but find information quickly, making navigation immensely important.

Once the audience for a site is determined, it is important to determine the functionality of a site. As such, testing is essential in order to determine that the overall form of a site is *useful*, that its audience can find what they require with a minimum of effort. This is not something that can always be done before web design begins, and we will deal with usability testing in more detail in Chapter 7, but such testing is not simply part of the post-production process: build in time to test your prototype along the way.

The structure of a site

Part of the planning process requires the web producer to outline the site's structure, how information is to be distributed across pages. The structure of a site is important: like chapters in a book or a storyboard, it serves a practical function both for the producer and the visitor to the site. For the producer, having a clear idea of the site's structure can establish the parameters for the most important information, whether there should be a link to a particular area (information about a company or individual, for example) that is accessible from every part of the site. For the visitor, on the other hand, a clear site structure can be useful in navigating through pages.

The first page is typically referred to as the home page, the starting point for the visitor. Another key term is a portal: while, strictly speaking, a portal serves as a gateway to other areas and services on the Internet (the most famous portals being search engines such as Yahoo and Excite), the entry point to a web site can itself be improved if it is conceived in terms of a gateway to that individual site. There are two choices here for the web designer: the first page may be a quick-loading and relatively information-free starting point designed to load as soon as the visitor reaches the page, or it may offer as much information as possible about the site.

If the first page is a 'flag' page, for quick access, any links to the home page in the rest of the site should actually refer to another page that contains more useful and relevant information. One way around this is to include important links in a frame that is never updated, allowing visitors to navigate more quickly to other parts of the site. A common mistake is to provide a series of pages with minimal information (and probably loaded with adverts) before reaching the important components of the site; while the temptation may be to keep visitors on a site for as long as possible, they may simply hit the back button on their browser.

After the portal or home page, a site is usually organised into 'top level' pages, which should represent the most logical organisation of a site. For example, a commercial web site may divide products into categories for sales, as well as provide support services and contacts. Top level pages should be available throughout the site, and do not represent the quantity of pages associated with a particular category: for example, individual products may constitute the main part of a site, but contacts, search engines and support links will also need to be clear.

As visitors navigate throughout the site, however, certain links to sections will become more relevant, others less so: if a visitor indicates a wish to read a

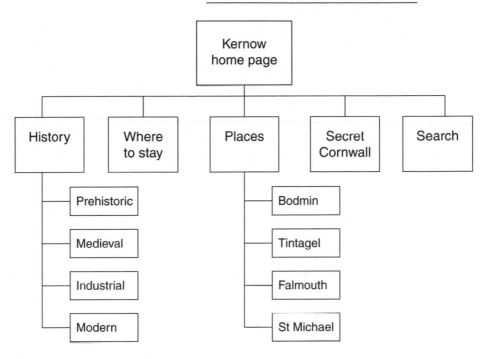

Figure 2.2   A sample web site structure

sports section, for example, selecting between football, cricket and rugby suddenly becomes much more important than when reading the international affairs section.

A quick and easy way to indicate the structure of a site is to create a tree diagram that constellates pages around their logical order. While this can be done with flowchart software such as Visio, at the very least anyone responsible for web production should sketch out the main areas on paper before beginning work on building the site. Figure 2.2 is a diagram for the sample web site we will create in Chapters 4 and 5.

Using a server

Setting up a server

While it is possible to develop a web site without using a server to test your design, some features of web production cannot be implemented without a server. In addition, if you are to be responsible for managing an Internet or intranet web site, using a test web server can prevent problems later on.

Setting up a server can be a complicated task beyond the remit of this book, but we will consider some of the options available if you wish to use a test server, paying particular attention to using Microsoft Personal Web Server (**PWS**). For many requirements, this will be sufficient and includes some advanced features offered by the Internet Information Server (IIS) provided with Windows NT and 2000, such as support for **ASP** (active server pages) and FrontPage extensions.

Microsoft products are not the only ones available by any means: probably the best all-round web server, one which is used on the vast majority of sites, is Apache (www.apache.org). It is available for platforms other than Windows (including **UNIX** and **Linux**) and, what's more, is free: it is also more complex to set up and administrate but offers more features than PWS.

Table 2.1 lists some common web servers that you may also wish to consider. For more information, go to serverwatch.internet.com/webservers.html.

Table 2.1   Web servers

Server	Platform	Price	URL
Apache	Unix/Linux/9x/NT/200	Free	www.apache.org
BadBlue	9x/NT/ME/2000	Free	www.badblue.com
GoAhead Web Server	Unix/Linux/9x/NT/2000	Free	www.goahead.com
Microsoft IIS 4/5	NT/2000	Free*	www.microsoft.com
Microsoft PWS	9x/NT	Free**	www.microsoft.com
TCL Server	Unix/Linux/NT/MacOS	Free	dev.scriptics.com
WebSite	9x/NT	$39 personal/ $299 pro	website.deerfield.com
WebStar	MacOS	$599	www.webstar.com

Notes
* with server versions of NT/2000
** part of NT 4.0 option pack

Microsoft Personal Web Server

While Apache and IIS require considerable technical skill involving setting up a network and administering the web server, a more common requirement is to run a server on the computer where the web site is being produced in order to test certain features which cannot be run from the browser alone. There are several personal web servers which are fairly simple to set up, but Microsoft Personal Web Server is widely available as part of Windows 98 (not Millennium Edition) or the Windows NT 4.0 option pack (you do not need to have NT installed to use PWS).

During installation, PWS sets up a default root directory for World Wide Web services and this is where the home page is found. To work with web pages, the Personal Web Server should load when Windows starts, and place an icon in the system tray in the bottom right corner of the taskbar. If it does not load, it needs to be started from Start, Programs, Internet Explorer, Personal Web Server and then clicking the Start button to make items available on a web site.

From the Personal Web Manager, directories can be added to a web site for different users, and this is where properties such as access and the ability to browse directories is set. Once PWS is up and running, web pages that are copied into the root web directory can be viewed via a web browser. If the part of the file address up to wwwroot, such as file:///C|/Internet/wwwroot, or C:\Internet\wwwroot, is replaced with http://127.0.0.1, a so-called 'loopback' address which directs the browser back to the server: the page will then reload with active, server-side information being pushed from PWS rather than called by the browser, with the result that certain features such as scripts and databases will be displayed, rather than saved elsewhere on the hard drive.

As mentioned before, you do not need to use a server for most aspects of web design, but it is worth setting up a personal server so that you can experiment with more advanced features. Some of the servers listed in Table 2.1 can also be used across a network if you have one, enabling you to create a personal intranet.

3
Pre-production
Online media toolkit

One of the virtues of producing for the Web is that, in comparison with other media such as print and broadcasting, it can be relatively inexpensive for the small producer once you have the basic equipment in the form of a personal computer and a modem. With the price of computers falling all the time and low-cost ISPs becoming more prevalent, it is possible to create sophisticated pages with little more than the text editor bundled with the operating system.

While it is possible to build a web site with nothing more than the tools included with an operating system, in practice producers will employ other programs, many of which are aimed at simplifying the task of hand coding a web site, others providing support for tasks such as video or image editing. There is a thriving market in tools to help web producers, many of them available as freeware or shareware on the Web (shareware programs are distributed freely but require users to register if the application is used after the evaluation period).

This chapter will outline the essential 'toolkit' for online production: not every application listed here is required – video on the Web, for example, still tends to be a specialised requirement – but the aim of this chapter is to be as comprehensive as possible. In addition to listing shareware and professional applications, in this chapter you'll be introduced to some of the terminology and techniques that every web producer should know about.

Web platforms and HTML

Browsers

After hardware, the first requirement to make use of the Web involves the browser which, as such software becomes more complex, raises the system requirements for computers. There are two main web platforms, Netscape (previously known as Navigator and Communicator) and Microsoft Internet Explorer. By the end of the 1990s, both browsers were neck-and-neck, but by 2001 IE had pulled far ahead despite the fact that Netscape is owned by the largest online media company, AOL Time Warner.

Despite the predominance of IE, these so-called 'browser wars' have had considerable consequences for web production and usage. While some commentators have welcomed such competition as stimulating development, the fact that browsers can interpret HTML in slightly different ways – even introducing proprietary tags – means that pages may display differently depending on whether the viewer uses Explorer or Netscape.

It is easy to assume that everyone uses either Netscape or Internet Explorer: indeed, the web statistics service, The Counter (www.thecounter.com) noted that of nearly 718 million impressions recorded in July to August 2001, 80 per cent were from visitors using Internet Explorer 5, 7 per cent with IE 4, and 10 per cent with different versions of Netscape. Nonetheless, there are alternatives, either in the form of new browsers such as Opera (www.operasoftware.com) or people with low-powered machines surfing the Web with older versions of IE, Navigator or even Mosaic.

The important point for producers is that content on the Web cannot be controlled in its final format in the same way that print or broadcast programs can be specified: the web browser used by the end viewer will affect the final product, and a considerable amount of time can be spent by developers testing their pages across a wide range of browsers. It may even be the case that two versions of a site are produced, one incorporating the latest effects, the other being a text-only site.

Testing a site, therefore, can be extremely important and, probably, the first part of a toolkit the web producer should invest in is as many different browsers as possible. While this book will cover issues of cross-browser compatibility, however, there will always be times, when using particular plug-ins or effects, when a choice will have to be made between compatibility for as wide an audience as possible and demonstrating a particular technology or using it for a specific effect. For example, the accompanying web site for this book, www.producing.routledge.com/pre4/index.asp, is designed to work with all browsers capable of displaying images and basic tables (such as Navigator 2); it does not look as aesthetically pleasing in such browsers, but text and links are displayed. The sample site that you will create in Chapters 4 and 5, however, will only work properly in version 3.0 browsers, and some features will not work in anything less than a version 4.0 browser.

HTML

HTML (Hypertext Markup Language) is the coding language used to create documents on the Web, the core component of any web page. Rather than being a full (and therefore complex) programming language, HTML employs tags indicated by angular brackets, for example <title>, to surround text codes: these tags are interpreted by a browser such as Mosaic, Navigator or Internet Explorer which control how the page appears. Usually there is an opening and a closing tag, the latter including a forward slash, such as </title>, to indicate when a particular tag ends. More importantly, HTML allows you to create documents that link to other documents on the Web – hence hypertext.

HTML tags may also include attributes that change the properties of a component on a web page; our title, for example, may include the attribute align= "center" to align it with the middle of a page.

HTML is defined by the World Wide Web Consortium (**W3C**, www.w3c.org) that sets certain standards governing how code can be viewed by any browser on any computer in the world. HTML 2.0 is an older standard: consequently, it is less sophisticated than versions 3.2 and 4.0 but is capable of being interpreted by older browsers. HTML 4.0 implements support for advanced **scripting** and better navigation and search capabilities, but pages designed for HTML 4.0 compatible browsers may not display as intended on earlier browsers.

One of the biggest choices facing web designers is how far to move away from raw HTML when designing web pages. Most new users have no interest at all in hand coding – after all, print designers do not need to understand PostScript to lay out pages for high-end printing processes. Nonetheless, although visual editors have increased in sophistication over recent years, a working knowledge of HTML is still recommended as even the best editors occasionally make mistakes with code that is easier to rectify if you have some knowledge of HTML. For more information, consult the appendix on HTML at the end of this book, as well as the course on learning basic HTML at www.producing. routledge.com/pages/htmltutorial.htm.

XHTML

Since January 2000, the version of HTML recommended by the W3C is **XHTML**, an adapted form of HTML using XML. The main difference made by XHTML is that rules now matter: previously, a web page would render even if there were mistakes, but in future such pages may not render at all.

XHTML pages must have what is known as a 'doctype indicator', an instruction at the beginning of the page that tells the browser what version of HTML it will use, as well as <html>, <head> and <body> tags. All attributes will now have to be placed in quotation marks (e.g. align="center" rather than just align=center), all optional close tags (such as </p>) must be included, nested tags must correspond and all HTML tags will be in lower case.

When XHTML is fully implemented, it will probably mean that the majority of pages on the Web have to be redesigned (see the section on 'Testing and Managing a Web Site' in Chapter 7 for more information). For this reason, browsers are unlikely to fully enforce the XHTML standard, but will continue to include backwards compatibility with older web sites for some time to come. For more details of the XHTML specification, visit www.w3c.org/TR/xhtml1/.

XML and XSL

HTML has developed greatly since it was introduced at the beginning of the 1990s, and is increasingly being used to achieve tasks for which it was not originally designed, ranging from creating help files to providing common file formats for such things as word processed documents. Recognising the shortcomings of HTML compared to these new uses, the World Wide Web Consortium introduced eXtensible Mark-up Language (**XML**) as a replacement for the stop-gap meta-tags that had been used to extend HTML functionality.

XML is closely related to **SGML** (Standard Generalised Markup Language) and provides web documents with the ability to be self-describing, whereby new tags are created rather like fields in a database. Thus the line <h1>Frankfurter</h1> is recognised by HTML as a heading, but could be either an inhabitant of the city or a sausage; using XML, the tag <location> can be defined to indicate the type of information contained in this tag, and this information then used with an XSL style sheet to display different types of information, rather like cascading style sheets (**CSS**).

XML is actually a combination of three technologies: the eXtensible Mark-up Language itself, eXtensible Style Language (**XSL**) style sheet descriptions, and Document Type Definitions (DTD) that enable XML documents to be passed between applications and organisations. XSL enables the manipulation of style sheets through scripting: as CSS1 and CSS2 describe how documents are presented, XSL enables 'user extensibility', that is a script for functions such as embedding a font can be written and attached to a style sheet. The potential for XSL is that it will clearly separate content from presentation, potentially speeding up production of web sites as writers can write content without having to worry about the appearance of a page.

Editing packages

Web editors

While we have discussed HTML, unless you wish to work very slowly (and very carefully) when creating a web site, you are unlikely to produce web pages using a text editor alone. First of all, page design often involves the use of such things as **JavaScript**, **Dynamic HTML (DHTML)**, **ActiveX**, and cascading style sheets that can be very complex when typing in a text editor. While inserting images and hyperlinks is, in most cases, straightforward, hand coding something like a table is more likely to create a headache than anything usable.

Unlike DTP or image editing, dominated by Quark XPress and Adobe Photo-Shop respectively, there is no clear market leader due to the open nature of HTML: at the time of writing, Dreamweaver is probably the single most important package that employers look for, but everything it does can be achieved in many other packages.

In addition, unlike print, where the producer distributes a version over which he or she has had more or less complete control, a web producer cannot guarantee the system on which their pages are to be displayed. This means that if a visitor does not have the font on your page installed on their computer, text will return to the visitor's default (such as Times New Roman), which will cause text to reflow in boxes on a page. One way to escape this difficulty in transferring documents electronically is by using a format such as Adobe's Portable Document Format (**PDF**) which embeds fonts and images within a page; doing this, however, can mean that visitors without Adobe Acrobat installed may not view your site.

A more common way of controlling some of the vagaries of design is to employ tables to lay out components of a page, and all current editors support this feature while most can also use frames and some style sheets which can simplify the web designer's task. Another element of web production that is not always addressed adequately is site management, but whereas only a few years ago this was something of a rarity, more and more applications now have in-built management features.

Below are some of the most common web editors: this list is by no means exhaustive, but covers virtually all the major commercial applications and some of the most successful shareware applications (see Table 3.1). Each one is accompanied by a description outlining its strengths and weaknesses, as well as its intended level of use. For a more comprehensive list, consult the *Web Production for Writers and Journalists* site.

- **Adobe GoLive** Originally GoLive's CyberStudio, this application gained a great deal of support in the Mac and is now available for PC as well as Mac. There is good support for more advanced features of web design, such as scripting, Dynamic HTML and cascading style sheets (CSS). GoLive's approach is slightly different to other editors: in addition to a visual editor it also offers a 'tabbed' view of HTML code similar to that in HoTMetaL Pro for designers wishing to edit tags quickly. Its main competitor is probably Dreamweaver, demonstrating some strengths (such as animation support) and some failings (site structure control) compared to that program.

- **Arachnophilia** Arachnophilia is a free web editor and one of the longest survivors, currently being up to version 4.0. Unlike many editors it is very compact, the download file being 1.6Mb, and it works as a text rather than a visual editor, highlighting tags in different colours to enable producers to edit them quickly. It can also be used to edit **Perl**, **CGI** scripts and even C++ and **Java** text very easily, with buttons and menus to add components to a page. There are also wizards for creating such things as tables, which can be very confusing to code by hand.

- **Allaire HomeSite** Recently purchased by Macromedia, HomeSite 4.5 is really an HTML text editor with some added visual features for page design and site management. The default view is of colour coded HTML, but it is also possible to transfer to a visual design view of pages. This particular application is aimed more at technical users, particularly those who wish to achieve more complex things in HTML. HomeSite's apparent strength lies in its support for the advanced aspects of HTML, such as scripting, ASP and DHTML, but these largely consist of useful tags for entering your own scripts, which is little more than other programs offer. It remains, however, a first class text editor.

- **McWeb Software Web Weaver** Web Weaver 98 is a shareware text editor that, like HotDog and Arachnophilia, has been around for some time and built up a considerable following, employing toolbars to add common components to pages. It also supports HTML 4.0, although not dynamic HTML elements, with wizards for such things as adding frames. The slightly more expensive 'gold' version includes a site management tool, 'Site Mongrel', and a CGI script to analyse web site usage.

- **Macromedia Dreamweaver**   An extremely sophisticated editor, Dreamweaver 4 is probably the closest thing there is to a standard in terms of web design. Pages can be edited entirely in visual mode, and Dreamweaver makes a very good job of making page design as close to DTP as possible. The program uses a series of floating palettes and windows, which can be fairly confusing for a novice although it can incorporate everything from JavaScript buttons to Flash and Java **applets**. As well as first-class management and automation tools, where Dreamweaver excels is in terms of its support for scripting. While requiring some experience to use effectively, it is possible to add JavaScript rollovers, pop-up windows and DHTML animations with no hand coding at all. The power of Dreamweaver lies in the fact that it supports advanced features as if they were basic: its interface is not the simplest to use, but it is currently the best editor around.

- **Microsoft FrontPage**   FrontPage 2002 is a powerful web editor that, aside from a couple of points, is also easy to use. It includes many features specific to the Microsoft Internet Information Server (IIS) bundled with Windows NT, which is beginning to be supported by more and more ISPs. To make full use of FrontPage extensions, you will need a server installed to view them. Site management features are fairly extensive, and you can view your site as a map or a visual display of links. There is also support for advanced features such as scripting and DHTML.

- **NetObjects Fusion**   Rather than present the user with a proliferation of toolbars, Fusion MX offers a Control Bar and Standard Tools Bar as well as a context-sensitive properties palette. The aim of Fusion is to simplify web design by standardising layout techniques, as well as offering decent web management tools. The Page view is where you lay out your designs and Site view the spot from where you create links and add new pages, with a Style section to speed up development. A problem with the application is that it is extremely difficult to edit your files in raw HTML if you need to (they are not saved in HTML format until published). As with Dreamweaver, however, it is possible to create Java-Script buttons and effects without any programming knowledge.

- **Sausage Software HotDog**   The unlikely-titled HotDog has been around for a long time, and although it is offered as shareware HotDog 6 is one of the most feature-rich text editors around. HotDog Express is

Table 3.1 Web editors

Program	Platform	Editor type	Site manager	Contact	Typical price
Adobe GoLive 6	PC/Mac	Visual/text	Yes	www.adobe.com	$279
Arachnophilia 3.9	PC	Text	No	www.arachnoid.com	Free
Allaire Homesite 4	PC/Mac	Text	Yes	www.macromedia.com	$95
McWeb Web Weaver 98	PC	Text	Yes (gold only)	www.mcwebsoftware.com	$29.95/$34.95 gold
Macromedia Dream-weaver 4	PC/Mac	Visual/text	Yes	www.macromedia.com	$265
Microsoft FrontPage 2000	PC	Visual/text	Yes	www.microsoft.com	$135
NetObjects Fusion MX	PC	Visual	Yes	www.netobjects.com	$99
Sausage Software HotDog 6	PC	Text	Yes (Professional)	www.sausage.com	$130
SoftQuad HoTMetaL Pro 6	PC	Visual/text	Yes	www.softquad.com	$129

a freely available beginner's package, but HotDog Professional includes toolbars and SuperToolz to add such things as DHTML and HTML 4.0 components to a page. While it is possible to do everything that HotDog offers in a simple text editor such as Notepad, like the best text web editors it simplifies many complex and powerful features.

- **SoftQuad HoTMetaL Pro**   HoTMetaL Pro 6 provides a graphical editor and, like GoLive, can also display the HTML tags, indicating where the editor inserts code in response to the user's actions. Site management features are excellent, providing a diagrammatic view of links and pages that can be scrolled through, indicating immediately clusters of links. HoTMetaL also includes a very useful validation tool: if this is left on, code is flagged on as soon as you enter an element that may not be cross-browser compatible, and it makes HoTMetaL a useful tool for checking pages designed in other editors. On the whole, however, this demands more technical expertise than the other visual designers.

For more information on web editors, see www.producing.routledge.com/pages/webeditors.htm.

Creating graphics

An essential tool for any web designer is an application to handle images: with some exceptions, probably most time spent on site development after producing copy is that devoted to creating graphics. Until very recently, PCs were from Mars and Macs were from Venus – and any poor earthbound computer user had to travel out in entirely different directions depending on which package they wished to use. For graphics artists, there was only one choice: the Mac, every time.

Since the introduction of Windows 95, however, competition has increased: many of the best applications are designed first for Mac, but ported very quickly to Windows. The Mac is still the chosen platform, but this is as much to do with the cumulative skills base of graphics designers working on Apple computers as any question of quality with regard to the PC. The image editors outlined below and in Table 3.2 concentrate mainly on cross-platform applications, as well as some shareware packages principally for Windows, but there are freeware editors, such as GIMP for Linux, which are also very powerful.

Image basics

There are two basic steps involved in capturing a digital image: sampling and quantisation. Differing intensities are sampled at a grid location and then quantised to pixel values on the screen, that is the intensity is calculated in terms of brightness of red, green and blue, and the result approximated to a number, or digital value.

This two-stage process is known as filtering. Another way to think of filtering, especially when used in scanning techniques, is as a finger sensing Braille dots at regular points on the surface before translating these dots into a coherent image. These digital values produced by filtering are then displayed as pixels. Each pixel is a discrete element of a picture, similar to the dots that you see in a newspaper photo if you look at it through a strong magnifying glass. The quality of the image depends largely on the sampling grid so that if it is too coarse valuable detail will be irretrievably lost.

Yet infinitely fine detail is unworkable across the Web. An $8'' \times 10''$ mono-chrome print at 600 dots per inch requires $4,800 \times 6,000$, or 28,800,800 pixels to appear completely smooth – approximately 3.6Mb: to record the same image in 256-shade greyscale requires 28.8Mb uncompressed storage space, and 24-bit colour (with eight bits per pixel for red, green and blue, offering a potential 16.7 million colours) would require 86.4Mb, or the equivalent of 500 copies of this book's text.

For images displayed on screen, resolutions are much lower, between 72 and 96 dots per inch (dpi). Similarly, compression of up to a half can be achieved with no loss of image quality, and compression between 1/10 and 1/50 can be achieved with no perceptible loss of quality. One reason for this is that an image will contain many of the same colours that can be described by a more compact algorithm; because no image can have more shades of colour than number of pixels (and very few images have as many as 16.7 million pixels), colours can be mapped onto palettes to save space.

Another distinction when dealing with graphics is between **bitmap**, or photographic images and **vector** illustrations, or drawings. While bitmap, or raster, images work by recording information about each pixel in an illustration, vector images use equations to describe the position and direction of lines on a screen. Thus, whereas a bitmap may have to describe each pixel that constitutes a line, a vector is defined in terms of two points and the distance between them.

The two main image types used on the Web are **JPEG** and **GIF** images, although there are other formats, some such as the Flash vector format being proprietary, others such as **PNG** (portable network graphics) open standards that can be displayed by the latest browsers without plug-ins. GIF images are restricted to 256 colours but are better at displaying large areas of a single colour, whereas JPEG files employ higher compression rates and display more colours, making them more suitable for photographic images.

Applications

- **Adobe Illustrator**   One of the great grandparents of the design world, Illustrator 9 from Adobe has long been the vector drawing package of choice for many graphic designers. Illustrator is really intended as the drawing companion to PhotoShop, with this program providing the tools to produce very complex objects, from basic shapes such as polygons and curls to controlling gradient colour fills.

- **Adobe ImageReady**   Designed to be used with PhotoShop, and sporting the same interface, ImageReady 2 is Adobe's image editor aimed at the Web. With ImageReady you can slice images to optimise file sizes and it supports GIF, JPEG and PNG-8/PNG-24 file formats for the Web. The program also uses layers to create frames for animation, with the final result being saved as an animated GIF.

- **Adobe PhotoShop**   PhotoShop remains the de facto standard for image professionals, and with version 6 Adobe has introduced extra support for optimising file formats for the Web. The Save For Web window is particularly useful and displays up to four previews of a graphic at different compression rates, so that it is easier to judge the trade-off between size and quality.

- **CorelDRAW**   The essentials of CorelDRAW 10 are the eponymous vector illustration package and its bitmap editor, PhotoPAINT, in addition to some other utilities such as CorelTRACE for converting bitmaps to vector images. Creating graphics has been made progressively easier with each release of DRAW, via such things as the Template Wizard, and it has a fairly intelligent (if overwhelming) interface. PhotoPAINT converts layers and images into masks that are easier to work with than similar layers in PhotoShop.

- **Corel Painter**   Painter 7 uses 'natural media' tools for recreating watercolour, oils, pencil, pen, and brush effects, as well as 'canvases', paper and cloth grains that react and blend to produce more subtle changes when used with different brushes such as chalk, paint and charcoal.

Table 3.2 Image editors

Program	Platform	Type	Animation	Contact	Typical price
Adobe Illustrator 9	PC/Mac	Vector	No	www.adobe.com	$399
Adobe PhotoShop 6	PC/Mac	Bitmap	Yes*	www.adobe.com	$600
CorelDRAW 10	PC/Mac	Vector/ bitmap	No	www.corel.com	$569
Corel Painter 7	PC/Mac	Bitmap	Yes	www.corel.com	$399
Jasc PaintShop Pro 7	PC	Vector/ bitmap	No	www.jasc.com	$99
Macromedia Fireworks 4	PC/Mac	Bitmap	Yes	www.macromedia.com	$299
Macromedia Freehand 9	PC/Mac	Vector	Yes (Flash)	www.macromedia.com	$599

Note
* Via ImageReady 2, bundled with version 6

Although other image editors have imitated these, along with its cloning tools, Painter remains one of the most sophisticated packages around.

- **Jasc Paint Shop Pro**   Originally a great success on the PC as shareware, version 7 of Paint Shop Pro offers vector image editing in conjunction with bitmap editing, presenting an application that is, for the vast majority of people, nearly as comprehensive as PhotoShop for a fraction of the price. The main virtue of Paint Shop Pro is that it flips easily between vector and bitmap drawing styles and supports a wide range of image formats, making it a good general image editor for the Web.

- **Macromedia Fireworks**   Fireworks 4 is an image editing package that concentrates on optimising graphics for the Web, using some clever tricks to slice images to compress them as much as possible, as well as offering a host of special effects as well as create image maps, animations and rollover buttons. Fireworks has been designed principally for screen- rather than print-based graphics, and its interface is similar to Dream- weaver, which it is intended to complement.

- **Macromedia Freehand**   If you are looking for a dedicated vector-based drawing package the choice probably still remains between Freehand and Illustrator. Freehand 9 integrates with Macromedia's other Internet tools such as Fireworks, Director and Flash, in particular using the latter to allow viewers to zoom in on vector images without loss of quality.

For more information on image editors, see www.producing.routledge.com/ pages/imageeditors.htm.

Interactivity and CGI

Most of the pages encountered on the Web are static, effectively consisting of pages that could be used in print medium with the exception of the occasional animated GIF and hyperlinks. Interactivity on such sites comes from naviga- tion controls and links, but more extensive interactivity can be provided in the form of changing elements in response to user input, such as search results from a database, modified displays when the mouse moves over parts of the page such as rollovers or drop-down menus, or sections of a page that can be moved around by the user.

Links aside, interactivity on the Web generally doesn't come from HTML but rather a number of languages and external objects that are embedded into pages, including JavaScript, CGI, Java applets, cascading style sheets, **Shockwave/ Flash** components and Dynamic HTML.

While static pages do not take full advantage of the Web, it is worth hesitating a moment before rushing to the other extreme and adding alert boxes or Java image applets simply because you can. For a start, such elements, especially if poorly designed, can slow down loading times; more than this, however, if they are overused and pointless, they may interfere with a site's overall design.

Dynamic HTML

Dynamic HTML is an important step for the next generation of HTML, but also an indication of the potential pitfalls that occur when competitors struggle to establish a proprietary rather than open standard. Both Netscape and Microsoft browsers support DHTML in their latest versions, but each uses a slightly different version, meaning that DHTML produced for Internet Explorer is not necessarily compatible with Navigator.

In its broadest sense, dynamic HTML brings together cascading style sheets and scripting tools, promising a finer degree of control over screen layout, more impressive interactivity and advanced multimedia features, and layered documents.

What DHTML does is introduce a series of tags that enable designers to control JavaScript and CSS elements on the fly, for example drop-down menus or hidden sections of a page. Dynamic HTML has the potential to be an extremely effective interactive multimedia language – it is, for example, much quicker than Java – but has been hindered by cross-browser compatibility. What this means for current designers is that they must often limit access to a site to one browser, produce two versions of the same site, whether for different versions for DHTML, or one version with and one without DHTML, or, more commonly, ignore it until compatibility issues are resolved.

Cascading style sheets

Cascading style sheets (CSS) enable designers to specify the appearance of pages through control of the elements contained within them, for example to display all level two headings a particular colour. There are two specifications for cascading style sheets, CSS1 and CSS2, which control text formatting and positioning respectively. To incorporate a style into a page requires the <style> . . . </style> tag with declarations and properties separated by a colon within curly braces, for example:

```
<style type="text/css">
H2 { color:blue}
</style>
```

The reason these are called 'cascading' style sheets is that they can be nested one inside another, with the one closest to the destination having most control. If a page were to have one paragraph in the Arial font, for example, it would look something as follows:

```
<p style="font-family:Arial">This paragraph in Arial
font.</p>
```

As the main use of CSS is to define overall styles for a site, the easiest way to use it is not to cut and paste into every page, but use the <link> tag in the header of a page to connect to an externally referenced style sheet, such as `<link rel=stylesheet type="text/css" href="pages/style1">`.

Layers

Style sheets can provide an overall definition of a site's appearance, but the most exciting potential development of dynamic HTML is layering – and the most disappointing because IE and Navigator implement different types of layering. Layers using the Navigator <layer> tag indicate the absolute position of a component using x and y co-ordinates relative to the left and top of the browser window.

Layering not only allows a component to be positioned anywhere on screen without using tabs and carriage returns, thus improving the appearance of a page, but also places layers one above the other. Not only can elements be positioned over others, they can be made visible or invisible, creating tabbed pages for example, that display different contents as visitors click on each tab.

JavaScript

Scripting is a way to extend the capabilities of HTML, particularly for dynamic feedback, the most popular version being JavaScript. This was originally developed by Netscape (under the name of LiveScript) but didn't really take off until Sun Microsystems took part in development and it was renamed JavaScript. JavaScript is recognised by most browsers currently in use, although versions of Internet Explorer prior to version 4 used Microsoft's VBScript and a variant of JavaScript called Jscript. Indeed, there remain some incompatibilities between Microsoft and Netscape implementations of JavaScript, but these are less serious than differences in DHTML and JavaScript is the most widely supported scripting language in use today.

HTML uses the tag <script> . . . </script> to include scripts in a page, which allows compatibility both with today's languages and any future ones, as indicated by the attribute <language>. Such scripts are interpreted by the browser and are part of a client-side process, rather than server-side CGI. Including JavaScript in a browser is very easy, although creating the script itself may be more difficult.

```
<head>
<script language="JavaScript">
<!-- hide script
"Insert your script here"
// stop hiding script -->
</script>
</head>
```

If you were using another scripting language such as VBScript (only supported by IE), the language attribute would need to be changed in the above example. Everything between <!-- and --> is ignored by browsers that are not JavaScript compliant.

JavaScript is an object oriented program, which means that every element on a page, such as images, forms and headings, can be defined as an object and named; once such objects are indicated, their properties can be changed so that, for example, check-boxes can be 'checked' or image paths changed to substitute them for other graphics (the principle behind rollover buttons). JavaScript also employs 'methods', or commands, to cause certain actions to occur on a certain event, such as a mouse click. For more information, see the JavaScript examples in Chapter 4.

CGI

Probably the most useful extension to web sites is CGI (Common Gateway Interface), a protocol built into HTTP that enables web pages to transfer instructions to applications stored on a web server. These instructions are processed on the server and the results sent back as HTML, for example notification that email has been sent or a form received. By providing a standard interface, CGI enables developers to use a wide range of programming tools to provide interactivity and process data.

CGI programs are often referred to as scripts because the first applications were written using UNIX shell scripts, commands similar to DOS instructions but considerably more powerful. It is possible to use programs such as C to produce CGI applications, but one worth learning because it is relatively simple and widely supported is Perl (see below). It is also possible to use CGI scripts that are pre-written and can be adapted for your web site. Such scripts must be hosted on a web server in a CGI script folder, and most ISPs already have basic CGI scripts for counting page hits or processing forms.

To be useful, a CGI script must be executable: the browser calling it must not simply be able to read it but also run the program. Some ISPs allow users to run programs from any point within their web directory, others, because of security issues, insist on running files from one directory only, usually CGI-BIN (for 'binaries'). Other ISPs, particularly free accounts, will not allow CGI access at all – because the program is executed on the server rather than the visitor's computer, CGI scripts can place a burden on the server.

CGI is usually integrated into an HTML document as part of a form, using the <method> and <action> attributes. These tell the browser how to send information back to the server and where the script is located. 'Method' takes one of two forms, 'get' and 'post': get appends the information to the end of the URL and is limited to a total of 255 characters, including the action URL, which can be a problem when collating information from a complicated form. Post, on the other hand, sends each value to the server and so has no character limitations.

For example, a common CGI line would appear as follows:

```
<form method="post" action="/cgi-bin/myscript">
```

In the above example, each value from a form is posted in turn and the information processed by a script which could email values to the web developer or generate a page depending on the results posted from the form.

Server-side includes

Another type of interactivity comes from Server-side includes (SSI, also known as Server-parsed HTML, or SHTML). Like CGI, SSI runs on the server rather than in the browser and can be useful for improving the development of a site. At its simplest, SSI tends to be used to standardise pages, inserting a button bar for example on every page: updates to the bar can be made by changing one file rather than having to edit the entire site.

Such SSI commands are embedded in HTML comments, similar to JavaScript instructions, such as the following to include a link to a button console:

```
<!-#include virtual="console.html"->
```

This command inserts the code contained in the file console.html into the page where it appears.

As well as simplifying site development, the main use of SSI and CGI is to take information passed from the browser to the server and process it. This can be used to collect information from visitors, to direct them to particular pages on a site depending on particular requirements and, increasingly, to sell goods across the Internet.

Perl

Perl, which has been described as the 'Swiss Army penknife' of the Web, stands for Practical Extraction and Reporting Language. Anyone seriously interested in producing fully functioning interactive web sites should spend time learning some of the basics of Perl: it is extremely powerful, is much easier than C to use – particularly as it lends itself so easily to customisation – and is present on just about every UNIX web server, as well as plenty of those running Windows NT or WebStar for the Mac.

Perl is an interpreted language, which means that code is not compiled for a particular platform but source code is converted to machine code on the fly each time the program runs. What this means is that Perl is slower than a language such as C, but it remains worth learning; on average, Perl is about 2.5 times slower than C but 10 times faster than Java. In particular, it can achieve tasks in one line of code that would require hundreds in any other language. Only for sites expecting tens of thousands of hits per day will Perl be insufficient.

The language is bundled with most releases of UNIX or Linux, and versions are available for Windows from www.perl.org. The following is an example of a very simple Perl script:

```
#!usr/bin/perl
#Generate a page of HTML showing date and time on
the fly
print 'Content-type: text/html\n\n';
print '<html><head><title>Hello world</title></head>\n';
print '<body><h1>Hello World</h1><br>\n';
# Display the date and time
print 'Date and time: ', scalar localtime, '\n';
print '<body></html>\n';
```

There are several features to note about the above script. First of all, comments are indicated by the hash (#) mark, and the first line (beginning #!) is important to indicate where Perl is located on the server; when customising a script, this may need to be changed to the actual path provided by the ISP.

Generated output is indicated by the command print, with the first line indicating the content type. The characters \n may not be required, but are used to indicate a line return on a UNIX server, and two returns (\n\n) provide a clear space between the content type and the remaining HTML. Preformatted output is indicated by the material between quotation marks, while the information generated on the fly, the date and time, is indicated by the instruction 'scalar localtime'.

One of the advantages of using Perl is that there are several sites, such as www.worldwidemart.com, that supply royalty free scripts that can be adapted for your own site. Rather than having to write a script from scratch, these files can be downloaded and customised for your new site; to simplify the task, many scripts place the information that needs to be changed as a series of variables near the beginning of the file, simplifying customisation even more.

ASP

Active Server Pages (ASP) is Microsoft's way of creating dynamic web pages as an extension to its Internet Information Services (IIS). A browser requesting an ASP page (indicated by the extension .asp instead of .htm) does not have the page returned directly; rather, it is parsed so that scripts are run on the server to insert new content, such as a database query, to the client.

Unlike scripting languages such as Perl, ASP is usually embedded within the HTML code for a page, and is indicated by the delimiters <% . . . %>, such as <% IF SESSION("username")="Jason" then %>. To create an ASP page, all you need is a text editor to write the code before saving it with the extension .asp, but many web editors also support ASP.

As well as server-side scripting to include information within pages, ASP can be used for routine tasks, such as storing data as a variable and tracking of visitors as they navigate from page to page, both of which are useful for passing information between pages, say for e-commerce.

For links to CGI resources, see www.producing.routledge.com/pages/resources_cgi.htm

Java and ActiveX

Java was developed by programmers at Sun Microsystems as a user-interface programming language called Oak which was supposed to revolutionise the way that consumers interacted with electronic devices. In 1994 (no one having bought Oak), Sun began to adapt it for the Internet and, in 1995, renamed it Java.

Java is unusual in that it does not run directly within the operating system of the computer but, rather, is operated from a software-driven 'virtual computer', or 'virtual machine'. The virtual machine is specific to the platform on which the browser is running, whether a PC running an operating system such as Windows, Linux, OS/2, a Mac or other computer such as a Silicon Graphics or Sun workstation. While this virtual computer is specific to the particular platform, however, the code that it implements is not, meaning that an applet can be written once and run across different computers without the need for recompiling.

If one of the golden rules of web design is speedy download times, loading a site with Java applets is a sure way to annoy users because most of them are not fast. That said, Java does offer certain sophisticated facilities, and the good news is that you do not need to be a programmer to use it. Programs such as Jamba and Director can output Java files but, for many of the most useful applets, you will need to use a programming tool such as Visual Café.

In addition, pre-made Java applications can be placed directly into web pages using applications such as Dreamweaver or FrontPage. Two of the best sites for Java applets are softwaredev.earthweb.com/java and the Sun site at java.sun.com.

Part of the excitement generated by Java was the fact that it did not rely on a particular operating system, which was particularly important to Microsoft's competitors such as Sun. Microsoft responded in two ways. First of all, it 'improved' Java to execute more quickly on Windows machines. It also promoted its own alternative to straight Java: ActiveX.

ActiveX is a set of technologies that ties together different functions and programs to offer web producers more control over how information is presented on a page. It is not really a competitor to Java in the sense that it is not a programming language, but enables other components, such as Excel spreadsheets, to be displayed via a browser.

Microsoft released an ActiveX Control Pad to help web designers create and use ActiveX components, but these have also been extended beyond the Web to other developments. The Control Pad includes a text editor, object editor for placing ActiveX controls directly into a document, a set of controls and a Script Wizard for adding scripts to pages. It can be downloaded from msdn.microsoft.com/fnf.asp.

For more information on Java and ActiveX, see www.producing.routledge.com/pages/resources_cgi.htm.

Multimedia

Audio-visual material can be entertaining and informative, but the Web was originally designed for text and the occasional image. As such, it has not yet fully developed into a broadcast medium, and is still struggling with issues around bandwidth, the amount of information that can be transmitted across the telephone wires and satellites that constitute the Internet. Full screen, all-singing, all-dancing sound and video is out of the question, so use audio and video carefully.

Internet video also utilises streaming, a means of providing audio-visual materials as quickly as possible. Rather than waiting for an entire file to download before beginning playback, streaming divides files into smaller packets of images or sounds that can be displayed almost immediately. The main AV formats are:

- **MPEG**   Small and fast but, particularly with MPEG2, capable of providing high-quality video as used in DVD.

- **MP3 or MPEG3**   Another highly compressed format used for sound which provides up to CD quality in smaller files and also provides for streaming.

- **AVI**   The Windows native format; capable of high-quality video but with large file sizes. AVI is not capable of streaming and is not supported on Macs.

- **WAV**   Sound file format, used primarily by Windows; can provide high-quality, CD sound but, without compression, results in large file sizes.

- **AU/AIF**   Sound file format similar to WAV, but native to the Mac.

- **WMV/WMA**   Windows Media Video/Audio, a high compression format from Microsoft that offers potentially high-quality video and audio.

- **DivX**   A hacked version of an MPEG4 codec that offers extremely high compression rates with little trade-off in terms of quality. The name comes from an unsuccessful DVD format from the late 1990s, and this is often popular on web sites trading films (legally or illegally).

- **RealVideo/RealAudio**   Popular formats on the Web, and capable of providing fast, streaming sound and video. Quality is not particularly high, however.

- **QuickTime**   Another high quality video format, and versions 3 and 4 also support streaming. Compression rates are higher with version 4.

- **Shockwave Audio**   An audio format from Macromedia which is based on MP3 to compress WAV and AU/AIFF files.

The most important rule for audio and video is that small really is beautiful. As well as reducing the size of video frames, if you are going to use AV materials on your web site consider packages such as Adobe AfterEffects or Equilibrium's DeBabelizer, which reduce frame counts or colours to make files as small as possible without destroying them completely.

Real media

RealAudio, released by RealNetworks in 1995 was something of a revolution at the time in terms of streaming data across the Web, meaning that users no longer had to wait for long downloads before they could begin listening to files, opening the potential for online radio and music channels. With Real-Video, streaming video also began to take off and, while the quality of Real media has been overtaken in the form of MPEG video and MP3 sound files, the RealSystem plug-in remains one of the most popular on the Web.

The Real plug-in can handle high quality audio as well as video, and also play other, non-Real format files such as AVI, WAV and even Flash. The plug-in actually consists of three parts: RealPlayer, used to download and play files produced with RealProducer software. Versions of these are available as free downloads, as is a limited version of RealServer, the web server software designed specifically to serve Real media using a proprietary **RTSP** protocol. While RealServer is no longer required to serve Real Media files, playback now being handled increasingly on the client (browser) side, the server is useful for webcasting, and offers multiple playback rates depending on the visitor's connection. Many ISPs now offer RealServer support.

The limited freeware version of RealServer (restricted to 25 simultaneous streams) is available from www.real.com, as are RealPlayer and RealProducer.

Flash and Shockwave

While most protocols for the Web are devised through a range of manufacturers or the World Wide Web Consortium, there has also been a thriving industry in terms of plug-ins, that is, third-party software used to display files incorporated into web pages that do not use standard HTML. Among the most successful of these plug-ins are Flash and Shockwave, developed by the multimedia company Macromedia.

Macromedia bought the application Future Splash, a vector-based drawing and animation tool that could produce very small files for downloading, and successfully marketed it to become the most successful plug-in on the Web. Flash has since moved on to become a tool with uses ranging from creating small animations and advertisement banners to complete interactive solutions.

Flash files are a subset of the Shockwave protocol, devised to enable web browsers to display interactive content produced within Macromedia's flagship product, Director. While preserving the interactive multimedia of Director files, Shockwave also compresses and streams files, that is, plays those files as soon as they begin to download and also enables files to be linked, so that only sections that are required are downloaded.

In combination with JavaScript, Flash is probably the most effective way of providing attractive and compelling interactivity to web pages while maintaining fast download times. Since Macromedia acquired it, Flash has been steadily enhanced and compatibility extended – Macromedia claims that over 80 per cent of browsers are Flash compatible, although developments to each new version of Flash mean that older browsers cannot play newer files.

Director, from which Shockwave files are produced, uses film metaphors to organise key components, with 'casts' (incorporating anything from a sound or image file to scripts and navigation components) that are arranged on a 'stage' according to instructions from a 'score'. While a difficult program to use, Director remains one of the best multimedia tools around and is more important than ever as Macromedia has targeted it increasingly towards the Web. For details on Flash and Director, as well as demos that can be downloaded, see www.macromedia.com.

4
Production
Designing for the Web

Web designers often rush in where angels fear to tread. We have spent a considerable amount of time on pre-production issues – selecting the appropriate tools, determining who and what a site is for, how it is to be developed – because it cannot be emphasised enough that time spent planning a web site will save hours further down the line.

Thus this book has outlined ways of thinking strategically about the Web, why you may be considering building a site and the tools and technologies you will need to create and manage your pages. The next step is to use these tools to construct a compelling web site, and this chapter will take you through some basic procedures of web design before moving on to dynamic content in the next chapter.

Before launching into web design, however, there still remain some factors that should be thought through when planning a site, particularly how it will look and work, how visitors will navigate through the site and what images, colours and text you will use. As such, this chapter will cover some basic design principles before going on to demonstrate web design in practice.

Design principles

Design is frequently thought of in terms of the appearance of a site – its aesthetics, how it looks. While this is very true and contributes greatly to the success or failure of a site, design is also a question of usability. Just as a chair may look great but be impossible to sit on for extended periods of time, or a car may blow away the competition in terms of its sleek lines but guzzle petrol like the villain in a Mad Max movie, so a web site that appears serene and sublime on the surface may leave visitors fuming with suppressed rage at best, indifferent at worst, if they cannot find what they want.

As such, this chapter begins not with the use of colour, graphics and other design elements such as typography – important though they are – but rather with the navigation of a site, how the visitor is to move around it and, following the precept that form follows function, make use of its contents. Finally, bear in mind that visitors to your site may not be using the hardware and software you have used to design that site, at the very least that they may be using a different browser.

Navigation

A well-designed web site does not simply consist of an aesthetically pleasing interface, but is also easy to navigate: or rather, the means to creating an aesthetically pleasing interface include paying attention to navigation as well as images and other design elements.

Good navigation depends on techniques for accessing the web site – interface design – as well as how the site looks. For example, users with slower connections may browse the Web with images toggled off, so text-only alternatives are a necessity: these may consist of a separate list of links, or using the 'alt' tag to include a line of text alongside the image. In addition, visitors with disabilities may not be able to distinguish certain colours or use a mouse to navigate sites, requiring sites to be accessible via keystrokes. For more information on providing access for users with disabilities, see www.skill.org.uk.

Navigation tools should, ideally, be consistent in terms of positioning and overall look and feel, as well as providing feedback to a visitor. If you change the position of a home page on each new page, browsers may become disoriented. Likewise, visually consistent navigation tools play an important part in constructing the image of your site. Regarding feedback, there are several simple and common techniques that are useful in providing information to users: it is common, for example, to include a greyed-out version of a particular graphic which is shown when a link is unavailable, such as when the link would simply take the user to the page already displayed; highlighting is also especially useful to indicate when a link can be followed, and this is probably the single most common usage of JavaScript on the Web.

While the types of web site may vary considerably, many share some common features. First of all, most sites open with a home or front page: like the contents page of a book, a good front page should provide some sort of overview of the different sections of a site, even if it's only links that enable visitors to see what is available: mapping your site is an important basic principle for successful navigation.

A common mistake when setting out these divisions is to lay out different sections in a radically distinct way, which can only serve to confuse visitors. A more successful technique is to implement the same basic design, with common buttons located in the same place, but change small elements of a page, for example a toolbar: this can help orient visitors within a site (they know that the page they are looking at is a news item rather than a review, for example), without unnecessarily perplexing them.

Text

While a considerable amount of time and energy will be spent on creating graphics for your site and making it compatible between multiple browsers, text remains at the centre of a web page: indeed, in the long term once a site is up and running and demonstrated to be usable, creating the content for your site in terms of words will probably demand most of your efforts. We will consider how to write for a web site in Chapter 6, but there are also some fundamentals that relate to using text for design.

At its most fundamental, text is fast: back in the days when users connected to bulletin boards using 300 *bits* per second modems, all they could reasonably be expected to look at on a bulletin board was text. For modern web designers, using text in terms of visual appeal can be frustrating: not only can users change the size of fonts (and, indeed, should be able to if they cannot read small text), typefaces may not even be available on a local system, causing the page to reflow in an unexpected and unwanted manner. There are means of overcoming these problems, for example by using cascading style sheets (which will be dealt with in the next chapter), or by employing download-able fonts such as Microsoft's OpenType (www.microsoft.com/typography) or Netscape's Dynamic Fonts (based on TrueDoc, www.truedoc.com), neither of which has become particularly popular as yet.

Typography obviously has a rich print history, which, it must be admitted, has not completely transferred to the Web. In this book, you'll often find refer-ences to fonts and typefaces as interchangeable, although strictly speaking a typeface is the style of type, such as Arial or Futura, while a font is its size, usually measured in points. Fonts are also distinguished as serif or sans serif, as well as proportional or monospaced. A serif font has a short start or finish stroke, while sans serif ones do not; proportional fonts use characters that take

Tips for navigation

Some of the most common navigation devices that work on the Web are as follows:

- **'Sidebars' and 'topbars'**   These provide consistent designs across a site, are usually visible and yet still allow room for content. Many commercial sites use combinations of sidebars and topbars, providing a top level view of content as well as more complex or specific links.

- **Frames**   Overuse of frames can be extremely frustrating for visitors, particularly those using older browsers and smaller displays. Used well, however, frames can be particularly effective for navigation where a producer wishes to display a consistent, unchanging toolbar that is downloaded once and thus speeds up the general performance of the site.

- **JavaScript and Java**   JavaScript is particularly useful for providing simple feedback to visitors in the form of rollover buttons that change shape or colour when the mouse moves over them. More complex sites may use Java or ActiveX components to create directory 'tree' structures.

- **Text**   Because images may not display as you intend, if at all, text alternatives are essential on a web site.

Some things to avoid when designing navigation for your site are:

- **Plug-ins**   With the possible exception of Flash, using buttons that require a plug-in is generally a bad idea. If visitors need to download that plug-in even before they can move through your site, the chances are they will never return.

- **Floating navigation panels**   While these may look very impressive at first glance, navigation tools that occupy their own window are easily lost behind other windows.

- **Java only**   While Java may provide some useful tools for navigation, older browsers may not display them, so provide alternatives. Also, while the most common use for JavaScript is to create rollover buttons, remember that you need to set up scripts so that non-JavaScript compatible browsers will not choke on them.

- **Redundant links**   Links to non-existent pages, as well as links to a page that the visitor is currently on, can be annoying.

up only as much space as they require, while monospaced fonts use the same fixed width for all characters.

Times: proportional serif font

Arial: proportional sans serif font

`Courier: monospaced serif font`

Typically serif fonts, by providing a little extra information, are easier to read for larger chunks of text, while sans serif fonts make bolder headlines. Monospaced text is not usually encountered – its principal use seems to be when designers wish to emulate typewritten pages or distinguish instructions within a web page.

Within a web page, changes are made to fonts using the <font> tag, which can be used to set a particular typeface, size and colour, for example, <font face="Arial" size="10" color="red">. Because text has been part of the Web since its inception, many simple formatting commands relate to text to make it bold or italic using tags such as <b> . . . </b> and <i> . . . </i>.

For a more detailed look at using text in HTML, consult the 'Hello World' tutorial on the *Web Production for Writers and Journalists* site at www.producing. routledge.com/pages/hello1.htm.

Graphics

Images are inserted into a web page using the tag <img> and the attribute src, which indicates where the file is located in relation to the page. For example, <img src="images/boat.jpg"> indicates that the file boat.jpg is found in a directory called images.

Using graphics in web pages is often a compromise between appearance and download times: the best looking site in the world is also likely to be the least visited if users have to spend too long downloading images. A realistic assumption is that most Internet users will be connected to the Internet with a modem capable of 3–4Kb per second, meaning that an optimistic download time for a typical 30Kb image is at least seven seconds. Overloading pages with too many graphics, or images with large file sizes, therefore, will deter visitors.

The primary rule for using web graphics is: compression, compression, compression. This is often a straight trade-off between file size and image quality, but using a specialised application such as Fireworks or ImageReady can make a significant difference by slicing complex graphics and compressing different sections at different rates. Also, bear in mind the virtues of the main graphic formats on the Web:

- **JPEG**   JPEG images make use of lossy compression (that is they discard information, flattening areas of similar colour into one colour) to compact an image as aggressively as possible. These are useful for full colour images such as photos.

- **GIF**   GIF images generally use lossless compression, whereby redundant colours are calculated by a mathematical formula. GIFs are restricted to 256 colours, and complex images such as photographs are usually larger as GIFs than as JPEGs; however, if you are creating images using large areas of simple colour, such as logos or buttons, GIFs can produce smaller file sizes and sharper, clearer images. GIFs can also be animated and display one colour as transparent.

- **Other formats**   Other graphic formats (which may not be supported by all browsers) include: Portable Network Graphics (PNG), images capable of preserving Photoshop-like layers, making them easy to work with, but combining some of the features of GIFs with high, JPEG-style compression rates and colours; the Flash, or Shockwave for Flash (SWF), vector format, discussed in Chapter 3; **Scalable Vector Graphics (SVG)**, an open format which, like the proprietary Flash format, can produce complex graphics with smaller file sizes.

One way to optimise graphics is by 'image-slicing': when an image is compressed as a single graphic, the resultant file makes a compromise between the range of colours to be displayed and file sizes. Preserve crisp, sharp images with a wide range of colours and the file size will be too large; on the other hand, reduce file sizes too much and the image will appear muddy and blurred.

Image-slicing divides the image into several different areas based on the ranges of colours used in the graphic. Each of these slices can be reduced to the smallest possible size but, because colours are within a certain range for each slice, the image should appear much clearer. Editors that support image-slicing will also produce an HTML table for reassembling the picture, which can be cut and pasted into another web page.

Another tip for optimising the speed of a page is to include the attributes height and width (measured in pixels) for the img tag. If these attributes are not included, the browser has to calculate the dimensions of an image before displaying it: while for a single image this will not be noticeable, for a page with several images it is worthwhile including these dimensions, for example <img src="./images/history_title.gif" height=50 width=150>, to speed up how the browser draws a page. To further aid navigation, also use the alt attribute: this provides an alternative text description when the image is not displayed, for example, alt="Link to history page".

For more information on using graphics in HTML, go to the Basic Hypermedia tutorial at www.producing.routledge.com/pages/hyper01.htm.

Working with colour

Simple but dramatic graphical effects are often achieved not by employing complex graphics but by the accomplished use of colour. Many colours are said to be complementary – for example yellow and black or blue and yellow, and a rather bland page can be improved dramatically by placing a colour logo or small graphic in a noticeable position. By contrast, using too many different colours, or colours that clash, usually makes a page look tawdry and difficult to use. Also, bear in mind that colour-blind visitors may have a problem distinguishing certain colours, such as red and green.

When creating graphics and using colour in web pages, it is often important to bear in mind the so-called 'web-safe palette', which consists of 216 colours. If you have any experience at all of designing for print, this range of rather garish colours will probably strike you with horror. Nonetheless, just as you have to take into account the fact that JavaScript and HTML tags may be incompatible with different browsers, so colours can vary from browser to browser.

While the very old computers capable of displaying no more than 16 colours are unlikely to be connected to the Web, a substantial number of visitors to a site may be using a machine capable of displaying no more than 256 colours. Although the computer you design on may display millions of colours, someone using such a display may see your beautifully designed graphics as an ugly shade of grey.

Some graphics applications save to a 'web-safe' colour palette, which consists of 216 colours. The reason this is only 216 rather than 256 colours is due to inconsistencies between the colours on Mac or Windows based systems: of the colours used by each operating system, only 216 overlap and are safe to use. Using any of these colours means that your images will display as intended on either system.

For computers displaying only 256 colours, images using colours outside this palette can be displayed in two ways: dithered (whereby two or more colours are mixed in a pattern, say white and red to create pink) or by converting a colour to the nearest shade within that palette. What this means is that, if you wish your graphics and colours to be viewed by as many people as possible, you should change your display settings to 256 colours to test your pages.

Colour crunching

Every colour is defined as a combination of red, green and blue values (RGB), and the number of colours that a system can display on screen is determined by the number of bits that it can support. Each spot of colour has one pixel each for red, green and blue, and the shade of the colour ranges from 0 (no colour) to 255 (the maximum amount of that colour). Thus black (no light and therefore no colour for that pixel) is 0 for each RGB value, while white is 255.

Many web- and image-editors represent colours as hexadecimals using two numbers from 0 to 9 or two letters from A to F (that is 10 to 15) to represent each RGB value. Thus black is 000000, while white is FFFFFF, unmixed red FF0000 and yellow mixing red and green FFFF00. You can find more information on colour and HTML at www.producing.routledge.com/pages/hello5.htm.

Regarding the number of colours that can be displayed, or the colour depth, increasing the number of information in the form of bits increases the range of colour exponentially. The smallest colour range is on or off, black or white, and is referred to as one-bit colour. More common are 8-bit colour displays, providing 256 colours, or above, or 24-bit colour with over 16 million hues.

Creating a site: basic features

Getting started

Having covered some general principles of planning, design and navigation, it is time to create a web site. As mentioned in the introduction, the set of tutorials that follows is not intended as a course in HTML, although you can find such a course on the accompanying web site at www.producing. routledge.com/pages/htmltutorial.htm. Instead, we'll begin with a very basic site that includes formatted text, links and images using three popular web

Design tips

- **Three golden rules for Internet design** Clarity, interactivity and download times. The most exciting and attractive site in the world will become a lot less interesting and attractive if users have to wait half an hour for pages to download. Visitors want a site that is a pleasure to use, simple to navigate through and loads quickly in their browsers.

- **Always consider your audience** Bear in mind that most people do not have a 19″, or even a 17″, monitor capable of displaying 1024 × 768 resolutions or higher, running the latest browser on the fastest PIII or G4 with a leased line.

- **Make your navigation controls consistent** Create a template design and then stick to it, so that visitors aren't confused as they move between pages. You may need different buttons on each page, but try to locate links in the same place.

- **Less is more** Don't overload your page with fonts, graphics and animations. Not only can these take longer to download, too many cause your site to appear messy.

- **Frontload important material** Visitors tend to work through web pages very quickly unless something grabs their attention, so you should place important material near the beginning.

- **Evaluate new technologies** Just because something is available on the Web does not mean that it is automatically worth placing on your site. Test new ideas and technologies before using them on your site.

editors: Macromedia Dreamweaver, Adobe GoLive and Microsoft FrontPage. If you wish to follow the tutorial for each application, you will also find them online at www.producing.routledge.com/pages/dreamweaver.htm, www.producing.routledge.com/pages/golive.htm and www.producing.routledge.com/pages/frontpage.htm respectively.

The site to be created on the following pages is a brief guide to Cornwall, its history, places to go and where to stay. Images and text for this site can be found on the *Web Production for Writers and Journalists* site at www. producing.routledge.com/resources.htm. To compare your work to the finished site, go to www.producing.routledge.com/kernow/default.html.

Before designing a home page, the first task is to set a root directory, a folder where pages will be stored. It is typical to place the home page here, along with one or two top level pages, but with other web pages and images stored in folders that will make the site easier to organise and manage. For the following steps, you will need to download the images and text for this tutorial from the *Web Production for Writers and Journalists* site at www.producing.routledge. com/resources.htm.

Setting the root folder

In Dreamweaver   Upon opening Dreamweaver, you will see three floating palettes, one for Objects, such as images and buttons, another for Properties, which change as different components are selected on the page, and a Launcher palette (if these are not present, go to the Window menu to display them). The last palette opens applications within Dreamweaver such as style and library inspectors, HTML editor and, by clicking on the Site button, a site manager.

After entering the Site Manager, go to Site, New Site and set the root direc-tory for your web site before creating two folders for images and pages. Copy the images downloaded from the *Web Production for Writers and Journalists* site into the former folder. The site manager is split into two screens, one for the site on a local machine, the other for the site on a remote server. Once a root location has been set, all pages and files will be saved in relation to this folder.

In GoLive   To set up a root folder, go to File, New Site, Blank: this displays a dialog box in which should be entered a site name and root folder; when these are entered, a directory is created and the site window displayed which, as well as offering a map of the site, also uses tabbed windows to set such features as font sets, colours and link management.

GoLive automatically sets up a home page, index.aspl. For page design GoLive breaks a document into a series of tabbed windows from which layout, frames, source code and outline (HTML tags) can be edited, with a final preview screen. Alongside this are two smaller windows: a tools Palette, from which components can be dragged onto the screen, and a Properties Inspector from which a component's attributes can be changed. As with Dreamweaver, you will need to create folders for images and pages.

In FrontPage   To create a site using FrontPage, go to File, New, Web. This creates a folder (including sub-directories for images and pages). FrontPage displays a number of templates which you can use to create a web site, but in this instance select Empty Web and click OK.

Working with colour, images and text

Having set up a root folder, the next step is to create a home page. Our home page will consist of a single image against a dark green background and a series of coloured text links leading to other parts of the site.

Changing colour

In Dreamweaver   Set the background colours and link colour for each frame to the shades of green #009900 and #99FF99, by going to Modify, Page Properties and clicking on the Background colour tab. You also change the title for the page (the text that appears in the blue band across the top of the browser), in this case calling it Kernow web site.

In GoLive   Setting background and text colours is more complex in GoLive than with any other editor: first of all, directly beneath the Layout tab is a page icon, which you must click on to display the Page Inspector. Go to View, Color Palette and from Tab I (for web-safe colours, version I), select the background colour #009900 and drag it into the box for Color on the Page Inspector, then select link colour #99FF99.

In FrontPage   Right-click and select Page Properties; click on the Background tab and set the background colour to green (#009900), then select link colour #99FF99 – to see this colour, you'll need to click on the More Colors tab.

Adding images

In Dreamweaver   Having set our basic colours, we now need to add an image, cross.gif: use the Insert Image button on the Objects palette or go to Insert, Image to place the cross on the page. Once the image has appeared, select it and click on the middle alignment button in the Properties palette.

In GoLive   To add an image in GoLive you must drag the image icon (indicated by the question mark) from the basic objects palette onto the page, then navigate to the appropriate file, in this case cross.gif. You can change properties for the image (size, border etc.) by using the Image Inspector.

In FrontPage   Add the image cross.gif by going to Insert, Picture, From File and navigating to cross.gif (you can also click on the Insert Picture from File button in the toolbar). To change the properties of an image, right-click on it and select Properties from the menu that appears.

Inserting and formatting text

In Dreamweaver   We have almost finished our first page, but we now need to add the text for our links. Place the cursor to the right of the image cross.jpg and press return twice before entering the text History, Places, Where to stay, Secret Cornwall and Search. As you enter this text, it should be centred on the page; if it is not, align it as you did the image, then select the text with the mouse and make it bold by clicking on the bold B in the properties palette.

In GoLive   Enter the text listed above under the image cross.jpg. To format this text, click the align centre and bold B buttons on the toolbar at the top of the screen.

In FrontPage   Enter the same text as for Dreamweaver and, as with GoLive, format this text by clicking the align centre and bold B buttons on the formatting toolbar.

Once you have changed colours and added text and an image, your page should appear as in Figure 4.1.

Using tables and layers for layout

We are now ready to create our second page, which will be linked to from the home page and also form a template for other pages. To make a slightly more sophisticated design, we will also use tables to organise images, text and links. More advanced editors such as Dreamweaver can also use layers to emulate DTP applications, but HTML 3.2 compatible browsers (such as older versions of IE and Navigator) can only display tables. While these may seem complex at first, they can be used very effectively to lay out components (the default for HTML being to run text and images from top to bottom), and indeed even the most advanced editors can save layers as tables for the sake of backwards compatibility.

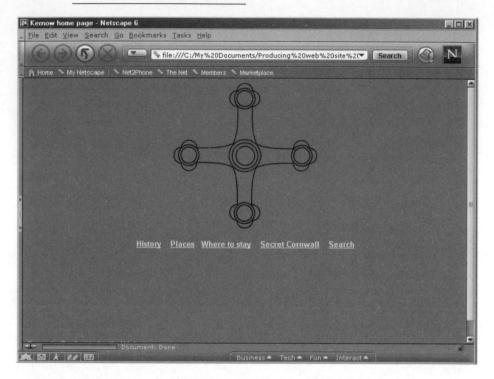

Figure 4.1   The first stage of the Kernow home page in Netscape 6

A table forms a grid in which text, images, links and other components are stored. Because each cell can be formatted individually, elements of a page can be aligned and arranged without changing the overall structure of a page. In addition, tables can be nested inside other tables, creating extremely complex pages. Before adding tables in your chosen web editor, create a new page with the background image backgrnd.gif and change the link text colour to mid-green that will complement the header.

In Dreamweaver With Dreamweaver designers can position content anywhere on the page by using layers, which function in a manner similar to frames and boxes in a DTP package such as Quark XPress. To use layers in the main editor, go to Modify, Layout Mode, Convert Layers to Tables. This will bring up a dialog box with four options: prevent layer overlap, show layer palette, show grid and snap to grid. The last two are relatively unimportant other than as aids to designing pages, while the layer palette enables users to select different layers more easily. Preventing layers from overlapping, how-ever, has important implications for page design. Browsers such as Internet

Explorer 4 and Navigator 4 and above can display overlapping layers, but earlier browsers cannot, so you should use Dreamweaver to reconvert layers to tables for backwards compatibility.

Insert a layer 620 pixels wide to hold a grid for the history page, then click on the Insert Table button in the Object palette to create a table two rows deep and two columns wide, with Cell Padding set to 1 and Cell Spacing to 5. The next step is to set the dimensions of the table for menu items on the left-hand side in a thin column. Shift-click on each left-hand cell then go to Modify, Table, Merge Cells. Finally, set the width of this cell to 100 pixels (leaving the right hand cells at 520 pixels).

In GoLive   As with Dreamweaver, GoLive can position page components using layers (called Floating Boxes) accessed from the floating Palette under the Basic tab; from here drag the Floating Box icon onto the page and resize the box to a suitable size before inserting a table. To add a table, drag the table button onto your page and enter the same dimensions of your table listed above, in the Table Properties box.

In FrontPage   FrontPage's layer tools are not quite as self-evident as in other professional editors, but they are there under Format, Position. This brings up the Position dialog box, which is useful both for wrapping text around images, and also – when you click on the Absolute Positioning Style for placing components in a layer that can be dragged around a screen as you require. To add a table, click on the table button in the top menu bar and drag across and down to create the number of columns and rows that you will require for your table, then go to Table, Properties to change its settings.

Understanding tables

Creating a table by hand is a laborious task but the importance of tables as a layout tool cannot be overemphasised. Even if you are using a sophisticated web editor with layers to drag and drop elements onto a page, for widespread compatibility with older browsers you will still need to save your design as a table.

Tables are contained between the <table> . . . </table> tags, these being used with several attributes including width (defined in terms of pixels or percentage of the window), align, border, cellspace and cellpadding. A table is a grid consisting of rows and columns defined by the <tr> . . . </tr> and <td> . . . </td> tags. The <td> or table data tag is used to define cells, and the number of cells in a row will determine how many columns the table has.

The table data tag is very versatile and uses a number of parameters to define each cell's attributes. First of all, they may span one or more columns or rows using colspan and rowspan, may align contents horizontally or vertically using align and valign, and may be formatted with different background colours and images.

A basic table would look as follows:

```
<table>
  <tr>
    <td>Row 1, Column 1</td>
    <td>Row 1, Column 2</td>
  </tr>
  <tr>
    <td>Row 2, Column 1</td>
    <td>Row 2, Column 2</td>
  </tr>
</table>
```

Using links

Once we have added a title, entered text for our pages, Home, History, Places, Where to stay, Secret Cornwall and Search, and created links to relevant pages, we will have completed our templates. Links provide the vital component for interactivity and are indicated in HTML by use of the anchor tag <a> . . . </a> surrounding the text or image which is the hot spot that users can click on to move between pages. The first anchor uses the attribute href (hypertext reference) to indicate the address of its target, for example:

```
<a href="http://www.yahoo.com">Click here to visit
yahoo</a>
```

Links may be either absolute or relative. An absolute link, as in the above example, is an address to a specific site on a server that must include all path information to that file, such as http://www.myisp.com/mypage.html, and is useful for creating links to external web sites. A relative link, on the other hand, is defined in relation to the current page. Thus inserting the image for the history page (history_title.gif) means that the link to this image is ../images/history_title.gif, that is the graphic is located in the directory called images. Directories and their contents are indicated by a forward slash, and to refer to a directory above the current one you must use two full stops.

It is best to use relative links for connecting to other pages on your site: if the directory which contains all your pages is moved, say to another ISP, the links will continue to work without any need for modification.

Adding links

As you add links in your web editor, you will need to use the following relative URLs for your site to work correctly.

- Home   home.html
- History   history.html
- Places   places.html
- Where to Stay   where.html
- Secret Cornwall   secret.html
- Search   search.html

In Dreamweaver   Select the text for each link and enter the appropriate page (home.html, history.html etc.) in the Properties palette. The target for each link, located beneath the link button in this palette, should be set to body so that each page loads in the bottom part of the screen.

In GoLive   Again, select your text and create a link by typing in the appropriate URL in the Text Inspector under the Links tab.

In FrontPage   Links are added in FrontPage by going to Insert Hyperlink or clicking on the Insert Hyperlink button.

To complete our template, in the narrow, left-hand column, type in the following items using bold text and hitting return twice between each one: `Prehistoric Cornwall`, `Medieval Cornwall`, `Industrial Cornwall` and `Modern Cornwall`. Select each one in turn and enter the following file names as links: prehistoric.html, medieval.html, industrial.html and modern. html. As we add pages to our site in the folder pages, these links will appear on every page and provide a quick link to the top level of the site.

Using the template

Templates provide a simple means of streamlining your workflow by creating a basic page on which common elements (background or other images, standard text, etc.) will appear. Another virtue of templates comes when managing sites: changing the appearance of an entire site can be laborious but, if every page is linked to a template, saving changes to this master file will update every page on the site. When you have created a table into which text and images can be inserted, and added common links for each page along the bottom and left-hand side, you can save this page as a template.

In Dreamweaver Go to File, Save as Template and give the page an appropriate title, such as MyTemplate. Going to the site manager will reveal a new folder called Templates in which this file is stored. When a template is created, the default setting is that sections cannot be edited so that consistency is ensured across a site. While our links will not be changed, the images and text entered into the main grid need to be updated for each page: to make this section editable, select the table holding these components and go to Modify, Templates, Mark Selection as Editable. Such sections will now appear in blue. To create a new page, go to File, New From Template and select this template: non-editable regions are now indicated in light yellow, but other sections of the page may be selected and modified.

In GoLive GoLive refers to templates as Stationery: once you have saved a page, go to the Site window and ensure the Extra tab is displayed by clicking on the arrow in the bottom left-hand corner if necessary. Ctrl+drag (Windows) or option-click (Mac OS) and drag your file to the Stationeries folder under the Extra tab to create a template automatically. You can now drag the icon that appears in Stationeries onto a new file to use the template.

In FrontPage Go to File, Save As, ensuring that FrontPage Template is selected in the Save as type box before giving the page an appropriate title. Going to the site manager will reveal a new folder in which the template file is stored. When you next create a new page, the template will appear in the New dialog box.

Once a template has been set up, the next step is to create the history subsection of our site using the template for five pages: history.html, prehistoric. html, medieval.html, industrial.html and modern.html. Text can be changed by cutting and pasting over the previous entries, while replacement images are selected by double-clicking on the picture and selecting a new file. Use the following files to change each page:

- history.html   history_title.gif/maentol.jpg/boats1.jpg
                     history1a.txt/history1b.txt

- prehistoric.html   prehistoric_title.gif/stone1.jpg/stone2.jpg
                     history2a.txt/history2b.txt

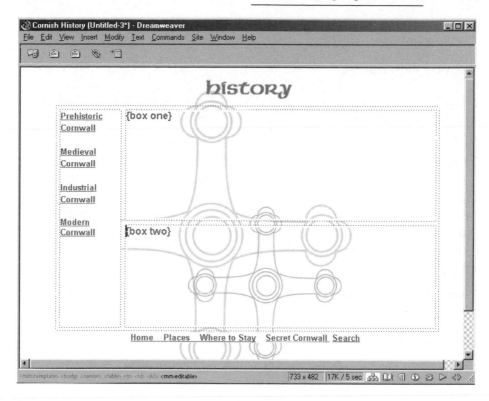

Figure 4.2   A Dreamweaver template for the Kernow site

- medieval.html   medieval_title.gif/church1.jpg/church2.jpg
  history3a.txt/history3b.txt

- industrial.html   industrial_title.gif/mine1.jpg/mine2.jpg
  history4a.txt/history4b.txt

- modern.html   modern_title.gif/beach1.jpg/beach2.jpg
  history5a.txt/history5b.txt

Note: as you add images to each page, select them in turn and, in the relevant properties palette or dialog box, set the alignment for the top image to right and the bottom one to left (so that text runs to the left and right of each image), and set the space around each graphic to five pixels so that there is a gap between each picture and text on the page.

Creating a site: Intermediate features

Working with frames

As well as displaying single pages, HTML 3.2 compatible browsers and above can display frames, that is, a single screen can be divided into a number of areas so that a side bar or header displays links to pages.

Frames divide the browser's display window into several areas, each one displaying its own HTML document. By default, these documents operate independently of the others, so that a link in one frame will load other pages into that frame, but it is possible to load documents into different frames, so that a contents bar down the left-hand side, for example, will display linked pages in the main window on the right.

The basic step for dividing a browser into frames requires the use of a <frameset> . . . </frameset> tag, which tells the browser to split the page vertically or horizontally into columns or rows. The frameset is kept in a separate document which loads other pages into the browser, for example:

```
<html>
<frameset rows="165,*">
<frame src="menu.htm" name="menu">
<frame src="body.htm" name="body">
<noframes>
<p>This web browser does not support frames.</p>
</noframes>
</frameset>
</html>
```

The above code divides the page into two rows, the first on the top 165 pixels wide, the second on the bottom taking up the rest of the page (indicated by the asterisk). Into the top part of the browser is loaded the page menu.htm, indicated by the SRC= attribute and given the name "menu", and on the lower part is loaded body.htm, given the name "body". The tag <noframes> provides a basic HTML page that is to be displayed if the browser does not support frames, displaying the text between the <p> . . . </p> tags. It would also be possible to include a completely different design here or, more commonly, a link to another page that does not use frames.

If the page were to be divided vertically rather than horizontally, the attribute cols would be used after frameset, rather than rows. Loading the page above displays the HTML documents with a distinct grey border between each frame. While there is nothing intrinsically wrong with using these borders, they can look very ugly, and so it is more usual to use the border=0 attribute to remove such lines from the page. This provides a region for an image or banner at the top of the page, and a menu bar down the left-hand side.

In addition to setting border sizes, the frame tag uses the scrolling attribute to determine whether that panel scrolls or not (set to no, yes, or auto depending on whether visitors can never scroll through a frame, must always scroll through it or will have a scroll bar appear depending on the size of the browser window) and sometimes the noresize attribute, which indicates that a frame's size cannot be changed. In addition, names can be assigned to different frames using the name attribute in order to enable inter-frame links: for a menu with a number of buttons, creating a link that loaded a page into the menu frame would remove the means of navigating around the site and would look dreadful. Using the target attribute, however, links can be made to load in a specific frame as long as it is named: thus a link on the page menu.htm would look something like the following:

```
<a href="page1.htm" target="body">
```

When creating a link to a page outside the site that is being worked on, target="_top" should be used, to load the page in the main browser window rather than a subsidiary frame.

Adding frames to our site

Before adding frames to the Kernow site, using the page home.html, we need to design the header that will appear above the home page. Create a new page and set its background colour to the same green as the home page, R=0, G=153, B=0. Save the file in the root directory next to home.html with the name header.html. We will insert a table with rollover buttons into this file later. For the top frame that is to be created across the top of our site, the size of the top is to be set to 80 pixels, with a border value of 0 and no resize or scrolling in the top frame (set in the appropriate properties palette or dialog box).

In Dreamweaver   To create a narrow frame across the top of our site, go to Modify, Frameset, Split Frame Up. This will produce a frame in the middle of the page that can be shifted to row 80 simply by dragging it up the page or changing the Row value to 80 in the Properties palette. From here, change

When to use frames

Frames are most commonly used to create side- or top-bar menus for navigation around areas of a site. It is important, however, in many cases to retain backwards compatibility with browsers that are not compatible with frames.

If accessibility is paramount, then it may be necessary to create a site without frames. However, it is also possible to update an existing site very quickly to display content with or without frames. First of all, take the main home page of the site (such as default.htm, index.htm or something similar) and rename it something like mainpage.htm. Create a frameset reference page that is then given the original name of the former home page – this will enable existing bookmarks to locate a site. Then, in the area of HTML between <noframes> . . . </noframes> copy and paste the source code of your original home page: if the browser cannot use frames, it will simply display the single main page. If navigation links are included here as well as in a menu bar, users will be able to use the site without ever knowing the difference.

Alternatively, a new version of the index page could be created, without frames, that enables visitors to view the site with frames or not (it may be, for example, that visitors with frame-compatible browsers would prefer to view a site without frames loading). Bear in mind also that visitors directed to your site from a search engine will probably load the page without frames.

the setting of Borders to Yes and set the value of the border to 0 to make the frame seamless. Simply clicking No may result in a white line between the two frames.

To save the page go to File, Save Frameset and give it the name default.html in the root folder. We must also provide these two frames with names so that our links can be set to target the bottom frame. Alt-click (Windows) or option-click (Mac) each frame in turn and in the Properties palette give them the names head and body.

In GoLive   To add frames to the home page, click on the second tab, Frames, in the main work space and then the fourth Frames tab in the Palette. From here, drag the third frameset that divides the page into a narrow header and large body frame into the Frames window and change the border size to zero. Click in each frame to set details in the Frame Inspector and Frame Set Inspector (click on the grey bar between the components of the frame to select the latter) such as frame size and scrolling. Name the top and bottom frames head and body respectively. Save the frameset by going to File, Save Frameset and give it the name default.html in the root folder.

In FrontPage   To add frames to our site, go to File, New, Page and select the Frames Page tab. This displays a number of frame templates: select Header. Ctrl-click to select each frame and then right-click to bring up the Frame Properties dialog box where you will enter details for frame size, border and scrolling. Name the top and bottom frames head and body respectively. For the head frame, right-click to bring up the Frame Properties box and type in the name, head; repeat for the body frame using the name, body. Finally, save the frameset by going to File, Save: give the frameset file the name default.html in the root folder.

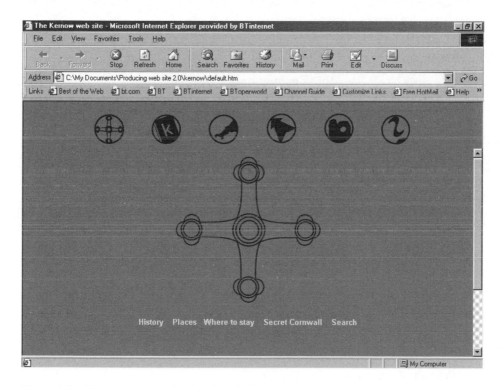

Figure 4.3   The home page displayed with frames

If you want to know how to hand-code a frameset, go to the *Web Production for Writers and Journalists* at www.producing.routledge.com/pages/tip_frames. htm.

Using basic JavaScript

Scripting is one way to make sites more dynamic, animating pages or components on pages, showing message boxes and collecting information to display different pages. JavaScript is a relatively simple scripting language compared to full-blown programming languages such as C or Pascal, but it is still complex compared to HTML with manuals and books devoted to teaching the ins and outs of JavaScript. In this chapter, we will concentrate on one specific example of how JavaScript works to create a rollover button for our site.

Using the hyperlink tag <a>, JavaScript can trap key mouse movements to trigger events, typically loading a new page or activating a rollover button. The sequence of mouse events are as follows (for PC users, only the left mouse button is supported by these instructions):

Event	Meaning
onMouseOver	Mouse pointer moved over object
onMouseDown	Mouse button pressed
onMouseUp	Mouse button released
onMouseOut	Mouse pointer moved away from object

Creating rollover images

One of the simplest ways of providing feedback to a visitor is to create a rollover image, which works by substituting one image, whether a jpeg or gif, with another. Such buttons can be made to work with most 3.0 plus browsers using JavaScript: when the mouse moves over the image, the replacement is substituted, when it moves out, the original image returns into position.

A basic script would look something like this:

```
<html>
<head>
<title>A simple script</title>
  <script language="javascript">
```

```
<!--
{ flashout = new image();
flashout.src ="flash.gif";
flashover = new image();
flashover.src ="flashover.gif"};
function picchange(imagename, newimage)
{ document.images[ imagename] .src
= eval(newimage + ".src")}
//-->
</script>
</head>
<body>
<a href="mypage.htm"
onmouseover="picchange('flash',' flashover')"
onmouseout="picchange('flash',' flashout')">
<img src="flash.gif" border="0" name="flash"></a>
</body>
</html>
```

The above script is divided into two parts: the header outlines the parameters of the script, identifying the script, providing a name ("flashout" and "flashover") for the images and identifying their source ("flash.gif" and "flashover.gif"): these names and the file names can be changed as required, but the rest of the script at this point should be copied as it appears above. PicChange is the JavaScript function, which is called in the second part of the script contained in the body of the page. To complete this part of the script, it is surrounded by <script> and </script> tags.

A rollover button must be attached to an anchor, though it is possible, as in this example, to link the page to itself so that nothing happens when a visitor clicks on it; more usually, a rollover button is used to highlight a link that does do something. The next part identifies the two JavaScript instructions – onMouseOver and onMouseOut – each of which swaps the current image (flash) for another (either flashover or flashout).

Next, the image source is identified and given a name: even though the image source is the same as the tag identified in the first part of the script, another name must be given for the image as it appears on the screen. This is a variable that can be substituted with another image source. If the name attribute is not included, the script will not work.

Adding rollover images to our site

Before adding rollover buttons into the file header.html, we must create a table one row deep by six columns wide, aligned in the centre of the page with the border set to zero, width 600 pixels and all the columns equal in size to hold each button. Each set of two buttons will be linked to the following page:

- home_button.gif/home_button_roll.gif   home.html
- history_button.gif/history_button_roll.gif   history.html
- places_button.gif/places_button.gif_roll.gif   places.html
- where_button.gif/where_button_roll.gif   where.html
- secret_button.gif/secret_button_roll.gif   secret.html
- search_button.gif/search_button_roll.gif   search.html

In Dreamweaver   Change the alignment of each cell in the table you created for header.html to centre and add the images listed above using the Insert Rollover Image button or by going to Insert, Rollover Image from the menu. The target for each link, located beneath the link button in the Properties palette, should be set to 'body' so that each page loads in the bottom part of the screen.

In GoLive   As above, change the alignment of each cell to centre and add images by dragging the Rollover button found under the Smart tab in the Objects palette onto your page. In the Inspector for each button, select an image for the button and rollover state, link them to the appropriate page in the URL section and ensure that target is set to 'body'.

Note: FrontPage uses Dynamic HTML hover buttons, which do not work in quite the same way as normal Javascript buttons. If you wish to know how to hand-code the JavaScript for the sample site rollover buttons, go to www. producing.routledge.com/pages/tip_rolloverbuttons.htm.

Creating image maps

The next page to add to the site is an image map. Image maps provide an additional means of linking documents: as links can be attached to text and images, so an image map defines a set of areas on a picture, each of which can be linked to a different URL. There are two main methods of creating image maps, the original image map which was devised for HTML 2.0 and is more usually referred to as server-side image maps and the HTML 3.2, or client-side, version.

Server-side image maps are supported by just about any browser that can display images but, as this involves configuring a CGI script, are used much less frequently than client-side maps. Although it is impossible to guarantee that all browsers visiting a site will be able to use a client-side map, the percentage of browsers incompatible with HTML 3.2 is negligible.

A map file is a series of (x, y) co-ordinates specifying the upper-left and lower-right areas of the defined areas of an image, with links to other pages. As with any HTML reference, it is possible to hand-code these co-ordinates, but creating an accurate image map can be incredibly difficult. If you are not using editors such as Dreamweaver, GoLive or FrontPage to create your site, there are several shareware and freeware tools on the Web, one that is particularly easy to use being Mapedit (www.boutell.com/mapedit/).

Before making an image map, create another file from your template called places.html, inserting the files places _title.jpg and map.jpg into the centre of the page.

You will also need to create the pages that the image map will be linked to, naming these as tintagel.html, bodmin.html, falmouth.html and michael.html and using the following text and image files which can be found at www.producing.routledge.com/resources.htm:

- tintagel.html   tintagel_title.gif/tintagel1.jpg/tintagel2.jpg
                       tintagel1.txt/tintagel2.txt

- bodmin.html   bodmin_title.gif/bodmin1.jpg/bodmin.jpg
                       bodmin1.txt/bodmin2.txt

- falmouth.html   falmouth_title.gif/falmouth1.jpg/falmouth2.jpg
                       falmouth1.txt/falmouth2.txt

- michael.html   michael_title.gif/michael1.jpg/michael2.jpg
                       michael1.txt/michael2.txt

Adding the image map

In Dreamweaver   An image map can be added to the picture map.jpg by clicking on it and selecting the rectangular map button in the lower left-hand side of the properties palette. The map buttons display a dialog box from which you can draw directly onto the image, indicating links to new pages. Draw a

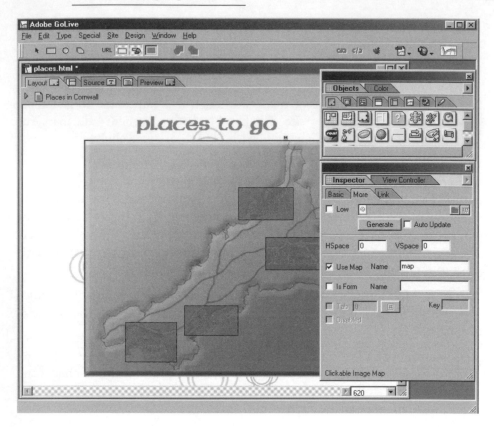

Figure 4.4   Using GoLive to create an image map

rectangle around each star and piece of text on the map and enter the following links for the four areas you define: tintagel.html, bodmin.html, falmouth.html, michael.html.

In GoLive   To add an image map in GoLive, you must first click on the image and then select the More tab in the Inspector and select Use Map. The toolbar then displays buttons from which you can draw directly onto the image. Use the rectangular tool, draw around the stars and text on image.jpg that you wish to transform into a hot spot, then, in the properties palette, enter the appropriate URL.

In FrontPage   An image map is added to the picture map.jpg by selecting it and clicking on one of the Map buttons in the toolbar at the bottom of the screen. As you draw onto your image, so a dialog box will appear, into which you enter the URL for the page that you wish to link to.

If you want to know how to code an image map in HTML, go to www.producing.routledge.com/pages/tip_imagemap.htm.

So far, you have learnt the basics of formatting text, using images and adding links to your site, as well as some more progressive features such as rollover buttons and image maps. The next step, which we will cover in the following chapter, will introduce you to adding more advanced components to your web pages.

5
Production
Dynamic content

One of the main virtues of the Web is interactivity. This is usually interpreted to mean feedback in the form of rollover buttons and animations; while important, interactivity can be implemented on web sites in a much more profound way, to process the information held on a site in response to visitors' enquiries. As such, this chapter will explore some of the ways in which content can be made truly dynamic on a site, using the common gateway interface (CGI) and scripting.

Not that dynamic content relies purely on technology. The most successful sites of this exciting new medium are those which offer some value added service, whether simplifying access to other sites as with portals such as MSN and Yahoo, offering searchable databases of news like the Guardian's Newsunlimited.com (www.newsunlimited.com) or the Electronic Telegraph (www.telegraph.co.uk), or simply providing a novel form of entertainment such as JibJab (www.jibjab.com).

Dynamic web sites

The web site outlined so far in this book is a relatively static entity: pages can be updated, of course, but the HTML files uploaded to a server will not change unless replaced. While this is more than sufficient to produce a great deal of useful content, dynamic web sites, which use server-based applications to respond to requests from the client browser and then generate a page dynamically have much greater potential. Such dynamic page generation can be as simple as including a page counter that changes each time the page is accessed, or as complex as processing forms, personalising pages and returning results based on output from a search engine or database.

Using CGI and server-side scripting

Building such interactive and dynamic web sites generally requires the use of common gateway interface scripts and programs. We have already looked at some of the processes involved in scripting using JavaScript, which is a client-side means of making web pages more dynamic, that is, the script is downloaded with the web page and interpreted by the browser. CGI, on the other hand, runs an application on the server before returning its results to the browser, meaning that pages can change in response to information from the user. One problem with CGI is that it can be quite slow: each response requires the web server to launch a program to process the request so that, with hundreds of requests, the server becomes sluggish. As such, server applications such as Java Server Pages (JSP) or Active Server Pages (ASP) are becoming more popular. These may not be much faster when launching for the first time, but as they do not need to initialise a program for each request they can handle a larger number of hits simultaneously.

Typical uses for server-side scripting include the following:

- **Forms**   Probably the most common use for server-side scripting is form processing whereby scripts take information from an HTML form, reading (or *parsing*) the data to post it to another user or an application on the server. Such scripts also usually provide a feedback page to the user.

- **Personalised content**   An increasing number of web sites are setting up personalised pages that can store the preferences indicated by visitors to those sites. For example, news sites will often provide links to sports pages for certain visitors, or political news for others. Such preferences are recorded either in **cookies** (text files) stored on the visitor's computer, or in a registration database.

- **Search engines and databases**   One area where the Web is extremely useful is for connecting web pages to databases, such as product catalogues or contact listings. At its simplest, a web site will include a search engine to scan pages on the site, but more complex databases will also allow users to organise and rearrange information, for example to list entries by date or location.

- **Security**   Security on a web site is, without scripting, a question of setting permissions on directories and files so that a visitor without appropriate permissions will receive an unauthorised access message. With scripting, however, visitors can sign up online and set or receive a password, which they can then also change at other times.

- **E-commerce**   One of the most important uses for server-side scripting is e-commerce. More or less impossible without server-side scripting, e-commerce employs database controls to access stock catalogues and also to process orders.

How CGI and server-side scripting work

When a browser requests a page from a server, it does not know a great deal about the documents it asks for, it simply submits a URL and interprets the information that is returned. The server supplies certain codes using the Multipurpose Internet Mail Extensions (**MIME**) specifications, which enables the browser to interpret different types of information – such as a graphic that is displayed or a zip file that is saved to disk. The server generally only sends documents and tells the browser what type of file is being transmitted, but it can also launch other applications. When a browser submits a URL that points to a file, the server sends back that file: when the URL points to a program the server launches that application.

Using the Common Gateway Interface (CGI) specification, the server can read and write data to disk, storing variables that may produce different results each time the application runs (for example with a page counter). Typically, documents on a server are read-only for the majority of users, with owners having the ability to write over the file – after all, there is very little point in developing a site if any visitor is able to delete its contents.

As well as read and write permissions, however, files may also have a third property, whether they are executable. To be useful, CGI files (often referred to as scripts) must be executed, that is they must launch, process data and, typically, write out the results of that process. Depending on the type of server, CGI files may be located in one directory, typically referred to as the CGI-BIN folder (from the days when all applications were referred to as binaries), or may be executed anywhere on the system. Typically, scripts are placed in one directory, as this tends to be more secure than allowing programs to be launched from any directory on the system. Before processing such data, however, it needs to be gathered which will require some sort of form on your web site.

Using forms

Netscape introduced HTML forms as a means of data collection across the Web, with information being processed on servers using CGI scripts. The form contains various controls, such as input fields and push buttons so that, when the 'submit' button is clicked a data string is sent back to the server. For this information to be processed requires access to CGI routines, but it is also possible to use simple mail routines to pass information on or to use JavaScript to send information between pages or guide a visitor to different parts of the site.

Creating forms

A form is an area of a web page defined by the <form> . . . </form> tag which contains the various input controls and fields added to that page, as well as other images and text. The most important optional attributes to the <form> tag are action and method, which, as we have already seen, control commu‑ nication between the form and the server using CGI.

Within these form tags can be placed six data control types: single-line text fields, multiple-line text areas, drop-down selection lists, push buttons, check boxes and radio buttons. For all types other than multiple-line text areas and drop-down lists (which have their own tags), each control is defined by the <input> tag with the attribute type=, followed by "text", "button", "checkbox" and "radio". There are also "submit" and "reset" attributes for buttons to send information or clear a form, as well as an input type called "hidden", which does not appear on a screen but inserts a string in any information sent back to the server – invaluable if it has to handle more than one form. Multiple-line text areas use the <textarea> . . . </textarea> tag, while drop-down lists are indicated by <select> . . . </select>.

When creating a form control, each one must have another attribute, name, a description that is passed back to the server or in an email. Some will have other attributes, including value, a default entry in a field or selected button, and size and maxlength (the maximum number of characters in a field). <textarea> tags must also specify col (columns), rows and wrap (to control word-wrapping). <select> tags must have an <option> tag for each item that is to be entered into a drop-down list.

If you want an example of the code for producing a simple form by hand, go to www.producing.routledge.com/pages/tip_simpleform.htm; for the complete code for the form for our sample web site, go to www.producing.routledge. com/pages/tip_complexform.htm.

Processing forms using Perl

To be more usable, the information from a form must be 'parsed', elements stripped out for processing by a form or email. If the server the form is hosted on supports Perl, a common way of doing this is to use the script formail.pl, available from www.worldwidemart.com/scripts/. This script should be hosted in the CGI-BIN folder and is extremely simple to customise. In a section near the beginning of the script, the user is asked to define variables, these include where the sendmail program (the UNIX application that posts email) resides – usually /usr/bin/sendmail or usr/sbin/sendmail – and the @referers field, that is the domain name of the server so that sites on other servers cannot use the script from your CGI-BIN.

To use formail.pl, the form itself requires some modification, particularly the addition of a field called recipient with an email address for formail.pl to forward the form results to and either 'get' or 'post' as the method to connect to the form, the address of which must be indicated in the action field. Thus the first two lines of our form above would look like:

```
<form action="http://www.myserver.com/cgi-bin/formail.pl"
method="post">

<input type="hidden" name="recipient" value=
"myname@myserver.com">
```

When the submit button is hit, formail creates a web page showing the information entered by the user which would be forwarded as an email like the following:

```
Date: Sat, 23 Oct 1999 16:45:08 GMT
To: myname@myaddress
Subject: WWW Form Submission
Below is the result of your feedback form. It was
submitted by () on Saturday, September 23, 2000 at
16:45:08
--------------------------------------------------
FullName: John Doe
Continent: Europe
Computer: PC
Submit: OK
```

Form design

Visitors' experiences of using a form are affected by various design issues, and it is easy to use forms inappropriately. For example, if users have to fill in several forms across several pages before information is collected and posted to the site manager only to be told on the last page that the information can only be processed in a different browser (and there is at least one e-commerce site I've encountered that does this), they are unlikely to repeat the experience.

In addition to considering design across a site, forms will be affected by page design, generally falling into the good, the bad and the ugly. Good forms, as in Figure 5.1, should flow logically between different sections, so that as a visitor tabs from field to field he or she will not be confused by a cursor passing backwards and forwards on the page.

A poor form, as in Figure 5.2, will break up the logical sequence of fields, as well as being difficult to read. An ugly form is better in that it is usable, but lacks character: to improve such a form is really a question of using tables and colour or graphics to spruce up the page – but only after proper data handling is established.

Adding a form to our site

The form on our site will consist of two sections: the first part of our page will consist of a list of three places offering accommodation, while the second will include a form requesting more information. In your web editor, create a new file, save it as where.html and add the title Where_title.gif to the centre of the page. Hit return and add a table consisting of three rows and two columns. With the cursor in the table, go to Table, Table Properties and set the horizontal alignment of the table to the centre and the width to 600 pixels. In each cell, add the following images and text:

- hotel.jpg/accomd1.txt
- self_cater.jpg/accomd2.txt
- bandb.jpg/accomd3.txt

We will now lay out a form requesting further details (which will be processed using formail.pl) beneath this table. When you create a table for the form four rows by two columns, you will need to add the following information:

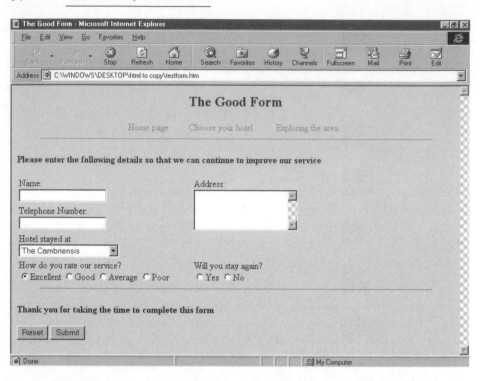

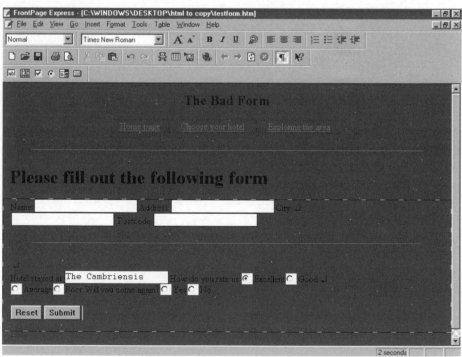

- Merge the top two cells and enter the text, For further information please complete the following form:

In the four remaining cells, ensure that the vertical alignment of each is set to top and enter the following text and fields:

- Row 2, left-hand cell: Name and Email, each with a one-line text box

- Row 2, right-hand cell: Address and scrolling text box set to four lines deep

- Row 3, left-hand cell: Season with four radio buttons labelled Spring, Summer, Autumn, Winter.

- Row 3, right-hand cell: Type of Accommodation and a drop-down menu. Double-click on this and select the Add button to add the following text to this menu: Hotels, Self-Catering and Bed and Breakfast.

- Row 4, left-hand cell: Two buttons, one to submit (the default), the other to reset the form (double-click on the button and select Reset from the dialog box that is displayed).

In Dreamweaver   To create the form, click on the top left-hand box in the Forms palette (if you cannot see this toolbar, click on the drop-down arrow next to Common and select Forms in the Objects palette). With the cursor in this form, create your table four rows deep and two columns wide. Select the top two cells and go to Modify, Table, Merge Cells for the caption requesting further information. In the remaining cells, add the content listed above.

In GoLive   Click on the top left-hand box in the Forms Palette and drag it onto your page. With the cursor in this form, create your table and select the top left-hand cell by clicking on its edge; in the Table Inspector set its column span to 2. Enter the content as listed above. The Forms Palette includes the fields that you will add to this table to create your form.

In FrontPage   Go to Insert, Form, Form. This menu also contains the other components that will be added later to create the form, such as buttons and text fields. Create your four by two table, then select the top two cells and go to Table, Merge cells before adding content as listed above.

Figures 5.1 and 5.2   Examples of well and poorly designed forms

Next we need to process the Form. There are two ways to do this. The simplest way to process the form is to send it as an email, and you can do this by entering `mailto:myaddress` in the Action field, with 'post' as the selected method. Alternatively, type in the URL of the formail.pl script if you have access to a CGI folder. If you are using formail, in the box Hidden fields you must click on the Add button and enter 'recipient' for name and an email address next to value: this hidden field will be submitted with the form and provides the variable for formail.pl to post on the information it parses.

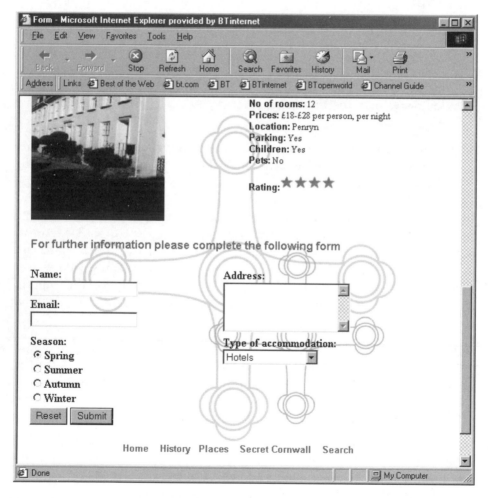

Figure 5.3   The Kernow web form

In Dreamweaver   Click on the red dotted line for the Form to select the Form Properties box and enter your email or the URL to formail.pl in the Action field.

In GoLive   Click on the small 'F' button to bring up the Form Inspector, and enter your email or the URL to formail.pl in the Action field.

In FrontPage   Right-click inside the form and select Form Properties. If you are using an email, choose Send To Email address; if you are using formail.pl, click on Options and, in Action, enter the relevant URL.

To complete the page, add links to the other top level sites. You may also wish to experiment with the page's format, for example by changing text headings to green to match the colours across the rest of the site.

Dynamic components and styles

Cascading style sheets

Cascading style sheets and current developments in XSL (eXtensible Style Sheets) are intended to distinguish between content creation and design in web production, with properties for such things as body text and links being established by style sheets; because these can be linked to as external files across a web site, it is possible to create a single file that, when modified, will adjust all pages linked to it.

Style sheets are only used by version 4 browsers and above, and Internet Explorer and Netscape Navigator implement them slightly differently. However, elements of a CSS file that cannot be parsed by a browser are simply ignored, so that font, size and colour revert to the browser defaults. There are two types of style sheet, type 1 which controls the appearance of fonts and type 2 governing the positioning of text.

A style sheet is a text file with the ending .css that can be created in an ASCII text editor; the next step for our site is to create a simple CSS file that will determine the format of links on pages. Open Notepad or SimpleText and type in the following:

```
A{ font-family:arial, helvetica, sans-serif;
font-size:10pt;color:black;}
A:hover{ color:white;}
```

Save the file as style1.css in the root directory, with default.html, header.html and home.html. The above file sets the font style, size and colour for any text contained between the tags <a> ... </a>. Note that style definitions are contained between two curly brackets, with each property being separated from its definition by a colon and each line ending with a semi-colon. The line 'A:hover' changes the colour for a hyperlink when the cursor moves over text, an effect similar to using rollover images. This (at present) only works in Internet Explorer, Navigator simply ignores this part of the style sheet. For the other pages on the site, save the file as style2.css and change the first font colour to green, the second (A:hover) to red.

The next step is to link the style sheet to our pages:

In Dreamweaver   Click on the CSS Styles button in the Launcher Palette or go to Window, CSS Styles. Double-click where it says (none) to launch the Style Sheet editor, and click the Link button to incorporate your style sheet into your HTML documents.

In GoLive   Click the CSS button in the top right-hand area of the main document window to open the Style Sheet window. Right-click (Windows) or control-click (MacOS) in this window to bring up a menu from which you can select Import External CSS.

In FrontPage   From the Format menu, click Style Sheet Links and select Add to link to your style sheet.

For pages on the site other than the home page, make the link to style2.css.

Search engines

One of the most useful features to add to a web site is a search engine, which, as its name implies enables visitors to search for items by entering a query. There are two main types of search engine encountered on web sites: the first allows users to search the entire Web and consists of a link to a major search engine such as Excite or AltaVista; the second, which is generally more useful, is a CGI interface linked to a script or a program running on the server which looks for matches to a query on the specific site.

Adding a search form to our web site

Designing a page for our search engine is relatively simple, in that all it requires is a text box, submit button and some instructions for use. First of all, open the file template.html in your web editor and replace the title with search_title.gif and the default table with one that consists of one column 600 pixels wide and is one row deep in the centre of the page. If your ISP supports FrontPage extensions and you have FrontPage, completing the search form is as simple as clicking Insert, WebBot component and selecting Search. This displays a dialog box from which variables such as labels and box width are set, as well as whether the results page indicates a score or file size and date. When you click OK, the page will be completed; when the file is transferred to the server, it must be placed in a directory that can execute scripts.

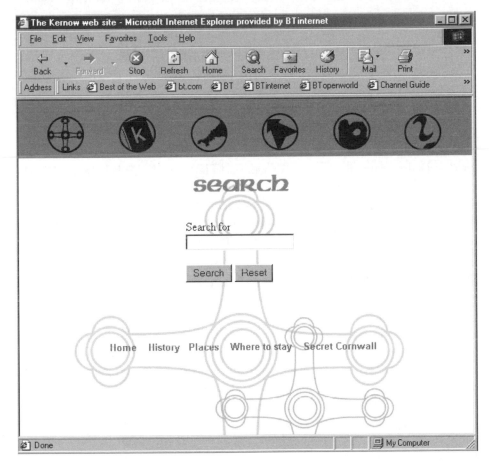

Figure 5.4   The Kernow search page

If your ISP does not support FrontPage extensions, there are two alternatives. The more complex, assuming you have access to a CGI-BIN folder and permission to execute scripts on your site, is to customise a Perl script for searching pages. Instructions for doing this can be found at www.producing.routledge. com/pages/tip_searchengine.htm. Not everyone has access to CGI facilities, so an alternative is to use a third-party search engine such as FreeFind.

You can find details of FreeFind at www.freefind.com. First of all you must register with FreeFind, providing an email address and site URL, before going on to customise your search engine, setting colours, fonts, etc. When you are finished, you complete the forms on the site and you will receive an email containing a password and the html that you can use to add a search engine to your form. This HTML can be customised further, but you will need to ensure that the 'action' tag for your form points to http://search. freefind.com/find.html, and that the 'name' and 'value' properties of your submit button correspond to those included in the email you receive from FreeFind. Once your code is added, you must tell FreeFind to 'spider' your site, whereby it builds up an index; this process can be automated to occur at certain times, such as the first day of each month.

Dynamic HTML

In the final section of our site, we will add Flash, video and dynamic HTML effects to create an interactive site. The first of these examples, for DHTML uses Dreamweaver and GoLive, and consists of layers which are used to hide and display information when a cursor is moved over a map: because these layers are not converted to tables, such pages will not display in version 3 browsers.

Dynamic effects, like JavaScript, are attached to events that can be triggered by mouse movements. As the events in this example are produced by the cursor moving over parts of an image, the image must first be sliced so that different sections can cause different effects. If you have a program such as ImageReady or Fireworks to hand, download the image penwith.jpg and open it in one of these applications: using mask tools, each program can create guidelines for splicing the image as well as generating the HTML code to incorporate the image within a web page. There are full instructions on how to image-splice using these programs on the web site under the techniques section. Alternatively, download the different penwith_r_*.jpg files and the file penwith_table.htm and cut and paste it into a template file named map.html.

The spliced image should be positioned in the centre of the page, with the file penwith_title.gif and links to each of the top level pages beneath it. The images contained in the table contain four yellow circles and four red stars corresponding to different places that display hidden text on the page.

In Dreamweaver   Using the Insert Layer tool, draw four boxes on each side of the map, copying the files penwith1–8.txt into each box. Once text is entered, select each layer and, in the properties box, set the visible setting to 'hidden'. It is generally easier to work with multiple layers if they are given distinctive names, and you can change the name for each layer in the properties palette.

After making each layer invisible, select the star or circle that corresponds to each one and select the behaviours in the Layers and Behaviors window. At the top of this window are plus and minus buttons to add and remove dynamic effects (or behaviours) to web pages. Click on the plus button and select Show-Hide Layers: a dialog box appears with the names of each layer and buttons to hide or show each layer. Select 'show' for each layer.

The default event to trigger dynamic effects consists of an onMouseDown event (that is, clicking the mouse), but pressing the small arrow next to onMouseDown will reveal a number of other events, including onMouseOver, which is the one needed to trigger a layer becoming visible. Objects may have more than one event associated with them: click the plus button again and this time select 'hide' for each layer, caused this time by the onMouseOut event. You could continue to add further events: for example, by carefully changing the colour of each circle or star, it would be possible to create rollover buttons that would light up as the mouse moved over them, as well as displaying hidden layers.

In GoLive   Using the Floating Box tool, draw four boxes on each side of the map, copying the files penwith1–8.txt into each box. Once text is entered, select each layer from the Floating Box Controller (View, Floating Box Controller or Alt+5) and, in the Controller, click the checkmark next to visible off so that they are hidden. To see the layers while you are working on them, click on the greyed out eye next to each one so that it appears with a red dot in the centre. It is generally easier to work with multiple layers if they are given distinctive names, and you can change the name for each layer in the properties palette.

After making each layer invisible, select the star or circle that corresponds to each one. First, click on the Link tab and then click on the Link button beneath URL to place an empty anchor tag around the image. Next, click on

Actions and, under Events select the trigger 'Mouse Enter'. Beside this box is a plus sign next to the word Actions; click this to highlight the button Action, which will display a menu when clicked. Select Multimedia, ShowHide, then in the boxes beneath this choose the appropriate layer and, for Mode, select Show. Do the same for 'Mouse Exit', but with Hide as the mode selection.

When you have completed these exercises in Dreamweaver or GoLive, save the page and preview it in a 4.0 compatible browser or later; it should look like Figure 5.5. As the mouse moves over the different icons in the central map, so different layers should become visible and disappear on the page, displaying text relevant to each part of the map. DHTML can be used to animate layers,

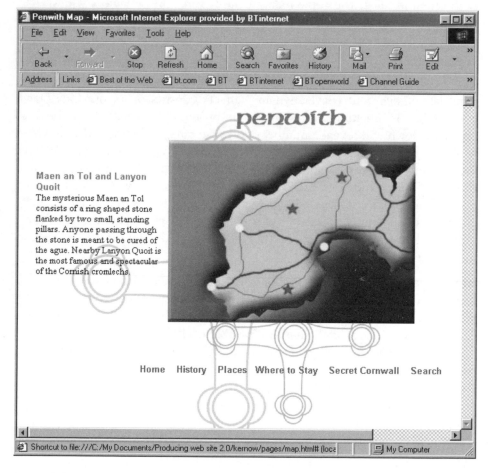

Figure 5.5   Displaying hidden layers with DHTML

moving them around the screen in response to mouse movements or clicks, as well as making different layers visible or invisible. The fact that Navigator and Internet Explorer implement such things as layers and other DHTML effects in slightly different ways, however, means that such effects are generally under-utilised on the Web because it is very easy to generate errors if a visitor is using a different web site. The moral is: if you wish to use DHTML, be prepared to spend a great deal of time debugging pages.

Flash

Macromedia's Flash has become an industry standard for animated and interactive vector graphics on the Web. Growing from a simple format for displaying images with animation, many designers now use Flash to provide a complete web interface: although it requires a plug-in to be viewed, this is widely available with most browsers and the program uses efficient compression techniques to provide small file sizes. What is more, although we will concentrate on using Macromedia's Flash to produce a small route planner, this could also be created in a number of alternative applications such as Adobe LiveMotion or CorelDRAW 10. This section will concentrate on the basics of creating a Flash component using files available from the resources section of the *Web Production for Writers and Journalists* site: if you wish to follow through Flash design in more detail, go to the tutorial at www.producing.routledge.com/pages/flash.htm.

The main parts of the Flash interface consist of the Stage, where you add elements to your movie, a Toolbox and the Timeline, where you animate your movie. You create a new movie by going to File, New and change its dimensions to 425 × 300 pixels at Modify, Movie. You can preview your work at any time by pressing Ctrl + Enter or going to File, Publish Preview. While Flash includes a number of drawing tools, you will probably find it easier to create graphics in a dedicated image editor such as PhotoShop or Illustrator. Import the background of our Flash movie, background.gif, by going to File, Import and then centre it on the stage. Align the files journey.jpg and places.gif with the left-hand side of the stage.

The easiest way to create an interactive Flash site is to add buttons which the user will press to take him or her to different scenes. In the Layer window in the Timeline, right-click and select Insert Layer or go to Insert, Layer. Double-click on your new layer and call it Buttons. With the buttons layer selected, import the image, button .gif: to make this into a rollover button, you must first convert it into a symbol to which actions can be assigned. To do this, go to Insert, Convert to Symbol and give the symbol the name Button 1, ensuring the Behavior for a button is selected. We can now change the state of the button when a mouse moves over it. Right-click on the button and select Edit, or go to Edit, Edit Symbols. In the Timeline, you will see four frames for Up, Over, Down and Hit, allowing you to assign up to four states to a button. We will only require two, so click on Over and go to Insert, Keyframe – a keyframe indicates when important changes occur to an object or animation. In this case, by importing and aligning the image button_roll.gif we can create a rollover button. Repeat this three times to create the buttons required for our route planner and add the following text using the T tool in the Toolbox: `Tintagel to Land' s End`, `Bodmin to Falmouth`, `Bodmin to Michael' s Mount`, `Falmouth to Land' s End`. You modify the properties of text such as font and colour using the modifiers beneath the Toolbox.

We have the basic building blocks for our scenes. Go to Window, Inspectors, Scene to show the Scene Inspector and, from here, click on the duplicate button four times and name each scene with numbers 2–5. You can navigate between scenes by selecting View, Go To, and selecting the scene you want. Go to Scene 2 and import the image tint_le.gif, then align it over the road between Tintagel and Land's End. Do the same for scenes 3 to 5 with the following images: bod_fal.gif, bod_mich.gif and fal_le.gif.

To make our movie interactive, we must assign actions to our buttons. First of all, however, we do not want our movie to play through each scene in turn, so we must stop it running through each frame. To do this, click on a frame in Scene 1 and go to Modify, Frame. In the tabbed dialog box that appears, click on Actions and then the plus button to add an action: select Stop to prevent the movie playing on. This is the same window where we will add actions for our buttons. Still in Scene 1, select each button in turn and assign the appro-priate action to it. For the first button, Tintagel to Land's End, for example, you want this to take the user to Scene 2. To do this, go to Modify, Instance and select the Actions tab. Click on the plus button and choose Go To, then, from the right-hand side, Scene 2, Frame 1. For each of the buttons in turn, repeat so that each one will send the user to Scenes 3–5 as in Figure 5.6.

Once you have created your movie, the final stage is to publish it so that it can be viewed as a standalone item or in a browser. Flash allows you to save movies as .SWF files that can be viewed in compatible browsers, standalone 'projectors' for Windows and Mac that require no other plug-ins, or as a series of images (GIF, JPEG, etc). To view these options, go to View, Publish Settings. In this case, we wish to save our file in Flash (.SWF) format, along with the

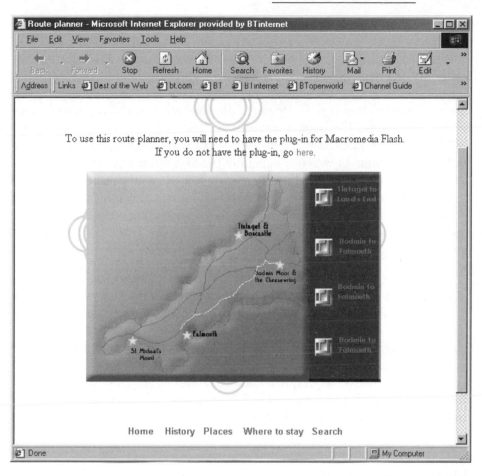

Figure 5.6   The journey planner created in Flash

HTML that we can cut and paste into a web page, so make sure both these options are checked and click publish. You now have the Flash file and HTML you need to incorporate this route planner into a web site, and the final movie should look something like the file you will find at www.producing.routledge.com/pages/flash05.htm.

Video

A complete guide to using video on your web site is beyond the remit of this book, but you should be aware of some of the implications of video on the Web. Most users do not have broadband access to the Web, so downloading large movie files can be an immensely frustrating experience.

When preparing video for distribution over the Web, therefore, it is important that you optimise your files for the correct size and compression. A common video size, for example, is 320 × 240 pixels: smaller file sizes suffer from 'postage stamp' syndrome, where it is barely worth viewing the file, but larger viewing sizes tend to increase a file size exponentially. Likewise, placing uncompressed video on the Web will result in huge file sizes, and just about every video editor available on the market includes codecs (compressors/decompressors) for QuickTime, MPEG or AVI formats. MPEG is probably the best bet as it is (at least for version 1) widely compatible but also offers a good ratio of compression to image quality. Other formats, such as Real or the new Advanced Streaming Format from Microsoft offer very high compression rates, although video quality can suffer. Finally, when preparing your video, consider the frame rate: moving images appear seamless to the human eye at speeds of around 24 frames per second, but depending on your requirements, you may be able to get by with 15 or even 12 frames per second, thus reducing file sizes even more.

Finally, optimising images is only part of the process of preparing video for the Web: audio contributes greatly to the final product, both as part of the perception of your video and also as it increases file sizes. As with images, experimenting with audio rates (typically from radio quality at 11 KHz to CD quality at 44 KHz), mono versus stereo and compression formats can result in a good compromise between quality and size, but be careful: obscure compression algorithms will result in visitors being unable to play your video unless they have the right codec pre-installed.

Adding video to our site

There are two ways to show video clips from your site. The simplest is to create a link to the file that, when pressed, launches the video in a separate player. Slightly more complex is playing video inline, that is as part of a page; this requires the user to have a player that can work as a Netscape or IE plug-in, such as Windows Media Player or QuickTime, which is much less of a problem than it once was.

In Dreamweaver   To add a video clip, first of all ensure that you have downloaded the file movie.avi from the *Web Production for Writers and Journalists* site. Create a new page from your template with the title movie_title.gif and save it as movie.html. Centre the cursor beneath the title and click on the Insert Plugin button or go to Insert, Media, Plugin. In the dialog box that appears, navigate to where you have stored the video file on your hard drive and select it. Finally, set the width of the plugin to 320 pixels and the height to 286. The actual dimensions of the movie are 320 by 240, but this will also provide room for playback buttons to display on the page.

In GoLive   Again, ensure that you have saved the file movie.avi to your hard drive and create a new page, movie.html, with the image movie_title.gif from your template. From the Objects palette under the Basic tab, select the Plugin button and drag it onto your page before navigating to your movie file in the Inspector. Set the dimensions of the plugin to 320 by 286 and ensure that the HTML option is set to <embed>.

In FrontPage   To add the file movie.avi to a web page called movie.html, go to Insert, Advanced, Plug-In and, in the Data Source field navigate to where you have saved your movie. Set the size and height of the plugin to 320 by 286 and click OK.

Customising Web-ready features

The CGI features discussed in this chapter usually require access to a CGI-BIN folder or FrontPage extension support. In many cases, however, CGI support is not available in this way (the web site is being hosted on student space or a free web-space server, for example). Nonetheless, third-party support often exists to make web sites more dynamic.

Links to servers hosting these features can be placed in a web page so that the visitor's browser follows the link. Thus a guestbook page may look like part of your site, but is actually being hosted on a completely different server. Many of these services are effectively free to the producer, being paid for by supporting advertisements. For more complete listings of such services, check the resource section at the end of this book and the resources web page at www.producing.routledge.com/resources.htm.

Content

The most difficult task facing any web producer is attracting visitors to a site and then encouraging them to stay once they are there. While well thought-out design features will entice such visitors to look at your site and good navigation will enable them to explore it more easily, anyone who stays on your web site will do so in the vast majority of cases because there is content there that is useful, interesting or entertaining.

We will cover the issue of content creation in more detail in Chapter 6, but it is also worth noting that there are several web sites that provide free content, usually as links to their own servers. The advantages of this for the average small producer is the ability to provide regular updates with very little effort and cost on his or her part: for the suppliers, such links count as their traffic and so help to drive up all important user numbers for advertising. There are a number of sites such as Multimap (www.multimap.com) and the Weather Channel (oap.weather.com/oap/index.html) that concentrate on a specific service such as providing maps or weather forecasts, but for a more general range of content go to iSyndicate (www.isyndicate.com) or the World Wide Information Outlet (http://certificate.net/wwio/).

When using these sites, you will need to register, usually little more than a name, site URL and email address. Services such as iSyndicate allow you to customise how information will appear on your site, although you will generally not have control over how the third-party content appears other than setting links to appear in a new window.

You'll find links to other sources for free content at www.producing.routledge. com/pages/resources_onlinecontent.htm.

Multimedia

Creating the right visual impression for your site can be time consuming but there are a number of online resources that can help. There are numerous sites where you can find royalty-free images (usually for non-profit use), for example at www.abcgiant.com, ls7-www.cs.uni-dortmund.de/cgotn and www. webclipart.com, and some of these also provide such things as sound files and even animations that you can use. You'll find URLs for more in the resources section at the end of the book and at www.producing.routledge.com/pages/ resources_multimedia.htm.

Generally, public domain images are probably less useful than ones you create for yourself from your own photographs. A more common requirement is for icons, rollover buttons and header graphics that will make your web pages more visually appealing and, again, the Web can be helpful in this respect. Button Maker at www.buttonmaker.com is handy for anyone who does not have a suitable image editor or the expertise to create their own title graphics and buttons, and you will find plenty of ready-mades at 3bgraphics. hypermart.net and www.coolarchive.com.

While we have looked at the basics of creating a Flash file, applications such as Flash and Adobe LiveMotion are complicated to use. If all you require is animated text, it is much simpler to use FLASHtyper, which you can find at www.flashkit.com, or the shareware program Swish (www.swishzone.com). Finally, if your web editor does not include tools for creating image maps, a shareware map editor is available at www.boutell.com/mapedit.

Guestbooks

A guestbook is a section of the Web where visitors can leave messages and view those left by other visitors. The HTML to display these messages has to be calculated by the server each time a message is added and then returned to the browser. As with many other third-party services, the link on your page is intercepted by the guestbook server and the appropriate data page generated.

There are various third-party guestbook servers, such as www.theguestbook. com, and www.glacierweb.com. Some of these can be customised with personal graphics and captions, and display banner ads.

Guestbooks tend to be rather superficial in terms of feedback, although there are times when a guestbook can serve a useful function as a focus for people sharing an interest. In general, however, forums are more useful. You'll find more links at www.producing.routledge.com/pages/resources_cgi.htm.

Response and search forms

We have already looked at the possibility of creating a search form on our site using a third-party search engine at www.freefind.com that sends out a 'spider' to explore your site before compiling an index and which is financed through the use of banners. Similar search provision can be found at everyone.net (www.everyone.net/main/html/index.html) and uptilt (www.uptilt.com).

Another useful function is retrieving information from users, for example collecting details for sending out purchases or information. While HTML forms are easy to create (see Creating forms above), providing feedback to visitors and posting on the information to the site producer requires server-side scripts. Typically, such scripts send the form to a specified email address, once the visitor has filled in all relevant details, and then sends a 'thank you' page to the visitor.

Once again, there are several third-party services that can process information for you, including www.freedback.com, www.responders.net and www. response-o-matic.com.

Forums and chat

Forums (or bulletin boards/newsgroups) provide the facility for visitors to a site to post a message to which other visitors can reply, building up discussion threads. Developing forums via CGI scripts is complex, but once again there is third-party support for forums, such as www.uptilt.com and network54.com. As with guestbooks, forum databases are stored on the third-party server: the link from a page is intercepted by this server that sends HTML back to the visitor's browser.

Internet Relay Chat allows people to exchange live messages that appear as messages in a scrolling window to which visitors can add their own comments. There are servers such as www.parachat.com that will host a chat channel for free with banners. When such pages are opened, the client is downloaded (usually as a Java applet usable with the browser) and connects to that site's channel on the server.

Although they tend to be complicated to set up, chat and forum areas on a site can encourage considerable feedback and tend to be popular with a wide range of visitors. If you are responsible for a web site, however, it is worth bearing in mind that it is easy for a forum or chat site to quickly leave your control if it is not moderated – that is part of the fun, but may be more difficult if you are running a web site for an organisation.

For more links to sites offering third-party support for search engines and forums, visit www.producing.routledge.com/pages/resources_cgi.htm.

6
Production
Writing, regulation and ethics

So far, we have concentrated on the technical aspects of site design, but technical skills alone do not make a successful site. Indeed, in the vast majority of cases, visitors to a site will not fire up their browsers and type in your URL to gape open-mouthed at how you implement the latest technologies; as with consumers of other media, whether it is print, television or cinema, their first concern is content.

Various pundits have suggested that, after the recent fallout, successful web sites of the future will be those that offer genuinely useful services or are content-rich. This is why media providers such as the BBC (www.bbc.co.uk), *New York Times* (www.nyt.com) or CNN Interactive (www.cnn.com) are placing so much of their content online. The idea is that, at present, users may be unwilling to pay for content, but when a fifty-year-old database becomes a fully searchable archive, the text and graphics we tend to treat as ephemeral are suddenly given a new lease of life.

Content creation

Setting the style

As well as becoming a content provider, successful web development also depends on developing an appropriate style for the presentation of material. Such a style depends on establishing an audience and cultivating a distinctive voice, and the basics of developing a good style cannot be repeated often enough: revise and edit your work and master the basics of punctuation and grammar. Demonstrating skills in DHTML and Flash may count for nothing if public perception of your pages is based on an inability to spell.

In many cases, the best style is often that which is clearest and plainest (though these are not synonymous). There is no reason why you should stick to such a style – after all, many world-famous writers are florid, metaphorical and elaborate – but if your desire is to appeal to as wide an audience as possible, you should write appropriately. As Matthew Arnold commented, 'Have something to say, and say it as clearly as you can. That is the only secret of style'.

Expanding on Arnold's advice, in most cases it is advisable to write as you speak but more precisely, to pay attention to rules of grammar and avoid colloquialisms unless they are relevant. Note, however, that simplicity in good writing is often more apparent than real, concealing painstaking art behind its artlessness. Indeed, clarity is often not the same as plainness; it can elaborate a subject but does so by avoiding jargon as much as possible.

In conclusion, then, the style must be appropriate to the subject: it should not rise above content, but is the means of expressing that content in as lively, clear and vivid a manner as possible. Sometimes a provocative and opinionated writing style may be the best way to attract readers. If you are writing copy for an online catalogue, however, you should be as self-effacing as possible, offering information clearly and succinctly to visitors.

Selecting an audience

All this leads on to the question of establishing an audience. For example, when publishing news (which has been very successful on the Web) there must be facts to report but, equally important, these must appeal to readers. One useful tip is to look at what is currently being published to see what is being offered. Remember also that a story is something that is crafted and also has an angle.

How do you determine a market on the Web? The first step should be to look at what is available across the Internet. There are many sites that offer some sort of editorial. Some of these, such as *Time* (www.time.com), simply offer the same material that is available in another medium. Others such as *Hotwired* (www.hotwired.lycos.com) or *Slate* (www.slate.com) develop original material that is aimed at a specific audience looking for material on the Internet. Do not neglect other media that offer a style or appeal to an audience you wish to address.

Many home pages or amateur sites offer factual information, a provocative stance on certain issues or locate other people who share similar enthusiasms. One of the virtues of the Web is that 'professionals' have not always staked out the relevant territory in advance; for example, in my own field of computer journalism, one site that gained a great deal of respect is Tom's Hardware page (www.tomshardware.com), which carries a large number of computer news and reviews and has even developed into a semi-professional venture generating revenue through advertising.

Crafting stories

News stories have been one particularly successful form of content on the Web. There are several reasons for this, such as the ability to update information on a regular basis, to search through stories and also the fact that news writing tends to pack a considerable amount of information into a relatively short space. While sites such as the Gutenberg Project (www.promot.net/pg/) perform an admirable task of transferring classic texts online, few people want to read *War and Peace* on their screens.

Such journalistic writing also offers some useful tips for developing a style appropriate for the Web: introductions to stories should be short and punchy, containing relevant information in the first twenty or thirty words. This 'news pyramid' traditionally enabled editors to cut stories from the bottom up so that important information would not be omitted. On the Web, this is made doubly important because readers may click on a link to a different page before finishing the story.

When developing such a pyramid, it is common to provide a brief statement that summarises the story, followed by a more extensive repetition of the intro-duction (often called the pivot paragraph which explains what the story is about) before finally expanding the details of the story in the main body of text. This is not the only way to develop a story, especially as a good story should have a dramatic ending, but on a web site it may be useful to extend the story over several pages rather than have one long page (particularly if there are images) which readers have to download before they can assess its value. Bear in mind that it can be much more difficult for most people to read text on screen than on paper: as a general rule of thumb, text that spans more than two screens may be tiring to read.

As Nicholas Bagnall has remarked in his book, *Newspaper Language*: 'Everyone knows the old saying: if you can't get their attention in the first sentence (or the first eight seconds) they won't bother with the rest.' At the same time, a web site should offer the opportunity to explore, to allow the reader to deter-mine their own pathways through which stories are interesting. A person who has bought a newspaper has, in some sense, already committed himself or herself to looking through it, however cursorily; the same is not true of a site on the Internet.

Surviving the burn

Five years ago, when old media companies began to catch up with new media entrepreneurs, it seemed that the web was going to set fire to communications in a way not seen since ... the last communications revolution. There was only one slight problem: while web sites selling products such as CDs, books and videos could (often with difficulty) persuade punters to part with their money, hardly anyone seemed willing to pay for intangible data, bits stored on hard drives as text, images or music.

For much of 1999 and even part of 2000, this didn't seem to be much of a problem: books such as Micheal Moon and Doug Millison's *Firebrands* (2000) indicated that the real secret to the new economy lay in establishing a brand that would blow away the competition, with almost inevitable profitability somewhere in the future. Unfortunately, it was only a matter of time before venture capitalists tired of what became known as the 'burn rate', how quickly dotcoms burned through investment money while failing to make any profit.

Figure 6.1   The BBC web site – not just surviving but flourishing

As such, many sites have suffered in the past two years or so: the sobering thought is that in many cases truly good content has not saved them, despite pronouncements by Net gurus that content is king. Sites such as *Suck*, *Feed* and *Plastic* have closed or scaled down; despite the evidence of much public interest in them, they failed to convince users and advertisers to invest in them. Not that it is all doom and gloom: sites such as that for *The Wall Street Journal* (public.wsj.com) have more easily persuaded readers that subscriptions are worthwhile, although 574,000 paying customers as of mid-2001 did not make it profitable. Others such as *Guardian Unlimited* (www.guardianunlimited.co.uk) or the BBC (www.bbc.co.uk) are using the Web strategically and effectively to deploy content created elsewhere or to support their other media.

Subscription is unlikely to become universal: even those sites that are relatively successful such as WSJ.com offer sections (such as opinion pieces) for free because they want these to circulate. Most sites will probably continue to offer free content aimed at hooking casual subscribers (and web advertising revenue, should it return) and charge for their archives, as many US papers do.

Storytelling techniques

Introductions to stories may consist of a narrative or anecdote, descriptive scene-setting, provocative statements or a quote or question. Endings tend to restate or refer to the beginning. The classic example is the detective story where the gun on a table in the opening paragraph is used to shoot someone in the final scene. It is not always practical to have a story that is so tightly plotted, but a good conclusion to a piece will progress ideas in the text as well as restating them.

A common technique is to include single line headings or descriptions with a link to the relevant story: if the reader is curious, he or she will follow that link. While it may seem unfair for your hours, days and weeks of work to be dismissed with a single click, an important technique for maximising a site is to create as many internal links as possible. Visitors will generally make their mind up about a page within a few seconds before hitting the back button or another link: if those links lead to attractive-sounding pages on your own site, you may be able to build up a wider readership than by insisting that visitors trudge through every page before deciding whether to stay.

Use boxes, bullet points, panels, sidebars and tables to offer information at a glance. Frequently readers will skim through an article looking at such things as pull-quotes (where a line of text is displayed in larger type), captions and boxes to see if the story is interesting before returning to the main body text. These various panels and boxes can summarise the information contained in an article or expand on additional information not dealt with in the main copy.

Prepare for an audience, but don't slavishly follow a formula – allow for surprises. There is no single formula that can cover every story, every article and review, every feature. Bear in mind that some of the most interesting articles will include information that the reader does not already know. Regarding writing style, the flow of content is important, especially if the text is fact-heavy, and one of the best ways of establishing whether copy flows is to reread material on a regular basis, to stop being a writer and *become a reader*.

Regulation and ethics

With the monumental growth of the Internet over the past decade, the rapid spread of international communication via email and the Web has brought its own problems and dilemmas for web producers, users and regulators. Over the next few pages, we will examine some of the main areas affecting regulation of the Internet and the ethics of creating content, paying particular attention to how these affect producers. Those looking for more information on general Internet regulation should also consult Jason Whittaker's *The Internet: The Basics* (2002).

The difficulties facing the regulation of an international communications medium have been demonstrated on a fairly regular basis over the past decade. In the UK, for example, the first draft of the Electronic Communications Bill was prepared to help build confidence in e-commerce and its underlying technology. Like the 1996 US Telecommunications Bill, this rather uncontroversial aim was overtaken by media interest in one section of such legislation. In 1996, it was the attempt by Congress to regulate online decency via the Communications Decency Act (CDA), in 1999 it was the attempt by the UK government to 'maintain the effectiveness of existing law enforcement powers in the face of increasing criminal use of encryption'. The right for police and other enforcement agencies to seize encryption keys was moved in 2000 to a Regulation of Investigatory Powers Act.

Because of its nature as a novel, international medium, the Internet in general and the Web in particular have raised questions about the ethics of its method

Tips for content creation

- **Select an audience**   While not necessary in the sense that you may wish to create a web site entirely for your own benefit and to express your own interests, having a clear idea of the audience you wish your site to appeal to can be helpful in terms of producing appropriate text and other content.

- **Write as you speak**   Or, to be more accurate, write as you would speak but more precisely. In most cases, this is the best way to produce clear, readable copy. Avoid jargon and aim for clarity.

- **Use the pyramid**   A technique from news journalism: offer a summary of your story at the beginning and expand from there. While this was useful to subeditors who needed to cut stories from the end, it is useful on the Web not to save space (which is almost never an issue) but for readers who may wish to move on to other pages.

- **Use links**   A good way to keep visitors on a site is to give them lots to visit. You can't guarantee to provide everything for everyone on one page, so include plenty of links to other parts of your site.

- **Become a reader**   Read and revise your copy on a regular basis.

of communication. Most of the debate has concentrated around the issues raised by copyright infringement, libel and obscenity.

Copyright

It has often been noted how suitable computers are for making perfect copies of information, whether text, images, audio or video. What is more, the ability to copy such data and transmit it around the world is open to anyone with a computer and modem. Previously international legislation, such as the Berne Convention of 1886 (revised 1971), and the Universal Copyright Convention (1952, 1971), has always approached copyright from the standpoint that significant infractions would be centralised in some way, and that copying via media such as video or audio tape would always involve some deterioration of the original source material.

Concerns over copyright infringements across the Internet prompted the European Parliament early in 1999 to propose the 'Copyright in the Information Society Bill'. The aim of this bill was to enforce copyright regulations, taking into account the ease with which data can now be copied. When the bill was first announced, it caused considerable consternation amongst ISPs because it excluded all copying, including temporary Internet **caches**, as part of the effort to protect copyright holders from Internet-based piracy. As the European Internet Service Providers Association (EuroISPA) lobbied for amendments, the bill was not passed in this form.

In the United States, the 1998 Digital Millennium Copyright Act and the 1997 federal NET (No Electronic Theft) Act have been instrumental in transforming and clarifying the nature of intellectual property in response to the perceived threat of the Internet, largely by forcing users to consider ownership of property such as data rather than material goods. The use of new (rather than pre-existing) legislation to pass judgement on possible copyright infringement has been limited so far, for example to a ruling in 1998 that software code is not free speech that can be published anywhere, in this case the code to crack DVD protection that was posted onto web sites and even on T-shirts.

A common assumption is that the ability to download something makes it freely available. This is not the case, although many people who break the copyright law on the Internet do so inadvertently. For example, a photo or article may be posted to a newsgroup without the original author's consent – even if the person posting the material is not paid for transmission the act may remain an offence although in most countries 'fair use' enables a certain amount of leeway to cite another source, though this is generally restricted to prose. Another misconception is that placing material in the public domain allows the producer to stipulate certain restrictions, such as free for non-commercial use only, or usable as long as no changes are made: content in the public domain can be used and transformed freely by users. This is why open source software, such as that associated with Linux, operates under the GNU Public License (GPL), also known as 'copyleft', which maintains copyright ownership but also allows users to copy and modify code freely. Finally, web producers concerned about maintaining copyright over their own materials should be aware that the law operates in the form of 'use it or lose it': turning a blind eye to minor infringements may lead to losing a case against larger ones.

One form of digital distribution that has aroused a huge amount of controversy recently is in the form of music, particularly MP3, where distributors have attempted to crack down on the illegal pirating of sound files. The most famous company involved in threatening the status quo was Napster, established in July 1999 by Shawn Fanning, who had written the file-sharing program while studying at Northwestern University. Napster, which operated as a **peer-to-peer** service, enabled users to log onto a server and see which MP3 files were located on the hard drives of other users; unlike similar services, such as Gnutella or Freeserve, Napster provided central dial-in servers to make it easier for users to find files (up to 2.7 billion downloads at its peak). It was this ease of use that also made it easy to crack down on Napster, and the site was forced to find new ways to deliver music services in mid-2001.

Responses to MP3 have generally consisted of attempting to introduce alternative formats that can be copyright-protected but, at the time of writing, these have not been particularly successful. Music piracy has long been an issue, with companies taking a percentage of the cost of a blank tape to cover anticipated illegal uses, but digital piracy is perceived as being a much worse potential threat because sound quality does not deteriorate with multiple copies. With regard to MP3 piracy, most small acts are not pursued – that is, should you copy a soundtrack from a CD into MP3 format on your hard drive you are as likely to attract official attention as by making a tape for the car. However, distributing that file to an FTP site on the Internet is a different matter, and attempts to regulate piracy have concentrated less on individuals than on the sites hosting illicit material. What this means in practice is that illegal MP3 sites tend to disappear very quickly and, increasingly, simply move to peer-to-peer links that involve no central server at all.

With regard to placing illegally copyrighted material on your own web sites, whether it is music, images or text, small cases may go unnoticed but it is not worth the risk of having a site closed down if you wish to use it for professional or commercial purposes. Although it is not impossible to regulate copyright on the Web the sheer ease and nature of digital copying almost certainly means that laws designed for older media will have to be rethought if they are to succeed in this digital medium.

Libel

As well as copyright issues, web producers need to beware of libel. Writers and critics are not immune to libel laws, and simply because you publish a web site without making a profit does not mean that you may not be taken to court. There is, however, a defence against libel in the form of 'fair comment'. This allows someone to be as harsh in their criticism as they like as long as it is honest opinion. In the US, the constitutional protection of free speech under the First Amendment has generally made for a much less harsh regime than in Europe (particularly the UK). The limits of a writer's right to free speech about public affairs were established in the 1964 case *New York Times* v. Sullivan, which set out that where the injured party is a public figure he or she must prove 'actual malice'.

The relative lack of prosecutions or settlements for libel has been taken to reflect the laissez-faire nature of the Web. Nonetheless, cases are on the increase and, particularly in the United States, have been influential in determining the role of the ISP although a considerable amount of ambiguity still remains.

Two cases, Cubby v. CompuServe (1991) and Oakmont v. Prodigy (1995), provided apparently contradictory evidence as to the state of ISPs, whether they are publishers of material or free carriers (rather like telephone companies). In the case of CompuServe, the court acknowledged the instantaneous nature of Internet postings and that it was not feasible for the ISP to examine every message. Exactly the opposite point was made in the Prodigy case, but this was due to the fact that Prodigy, a family-oriented service, specifically claimed to regulate the contents of its bulletin boards. An ironic consequence, in the US at least, is that ISPs increasingly do not regulate bulletin board postings at all to avoid being liable as publishers, something reinforced by two more recent cases: Zeran v. America Online (1997) established that AOL could not be held negligent in delaying the removal of defamatory messages, while Lunney v. Prodigy (2000) saw the US Supreme Court rule that ISPs have full protection against libellous or abusive email postings over the Web, after a former boy scout served Prodigy with a lawsuit following postings of threatening messages by an impostor using his name.

In the UK, the 1996 Defamation Act attempted to clarify the position of ISPs as secondary carriers, whereby if the ISP demonstrates that due care is taken to monitor content it is not liable, a so-called 'Section 1' defence. This can also be employed in line with other defences by a publisher, such as fair comment, justification and privilege. Rather than encourage a hands-off approach, the Act attempts to encourage ISPs to monitor postings while accepting the impossibility of checking them all.

Until 1999, there had been little significant legislation concerning libellous statements on the Internet in the UK, though some figures had received out-of-court settlements for statements circulated on email or news groups. For example, Norwich Union agreed to pay the Western Provident Association (WPA) £450,000 for comments made in an internal email that, WPA argued, was defamatory. Dr Laurence Godfrey filed a more serious suit against Demon in 1999, after defamatory remarks had been posted to a newsgroup hosted on a Demon server. It was held immaterial whether Dr Godfrey or the poster were Demon customers, the key point being Demon's refusal to remove the posting once Dr Godfrey had complained to the ISP about it. The case was also complicated by the fact that the posting was anonymous, meaning the plaintiff could not pursue the author.

While this particular case affected an ISP, libel is also an issue for web publishers, more so in that the defence of being a free carrier is not open to them. In many cases, web publishing can follow straightforward defamation rules for print and other media, but where a bulletin board, for example, is included on a web site, it is the producer's responsibility to manage this as much as is possible, meaning that postings must be monitored and, more importantly, a complaint-handling procedure should be in place. Should a complaint be received, access to the offending message should be *suspended* (the message does not need to be deleted) until it is assessed and a response made to the complainant, ideally within 24 hours.

It is also advisable to make clear limits of acceptable behaviour on a web site, particularly as to what material will be removed. The difficulties of monitoring the millions of web sites stored on many ISPs' servers has also been recognised in a recent ruling by Dame Elizabeth Butler-Sloss, who had placed an injunction against the British media revealing the new identities of the killers of Jamie Bulger. In July 2001, after clarification was sought by an understandably nervous Demon, she ruled that her original injunction could not apply in its original form to ISPs.

When using the defence of fair comment for information placed on a web site by the producer, rather than a third party, it is important to get the facts right: opinion is not the same as fact, so that saying an item is too expensive and then quoting the wrong price will not be helpful if you are later sued. Second, and this is often the most difficult part of defending against libel, an opinion that is judged excessive – such as calling someone obese who has put on a couple of pounds – may not be held to be honest opinion. Likewise, if there is a chance that your writing may be motivated by malice, such as a review of work by your ex-partner, it is probably advisable not to publish.

The last test of honest opinion is whether a piece of work is in the public interest. If you are writing about something that has been published or distributed such as a book, interview or film, then this is usually less of a problem than reciting gossip about a figure who may not be in the public domain.

Obscenity

For most web designers, copyright will be the largest problem when creating content. However, part of the excitement of the Internet revolves around its status as the largest uncensored mass medium in history. Scare stories of paedophilia, terrorism and racism abound on the Internet or, more usually, in other media discussing the Internet. There are unsavoury, and even criminal, sites on the Web, but not necessarily to the saturation point indicated by such stories.

In 1996, responding to these stories, the US Government attempted to control the publication of obscene material on the Internet by means of the Communications Decency Act, part of a wider telecommunications bill. This proved to be a rather draconian and heavy-handed regulatory tool in that the letter of the law applied more excessive regulation against the Web than for any other medium, with the Act being declared unconstitutional within months. In the UK, the 1990 Computer Misuse Act and notoriously slippery 1959 Obscene Publications Act (OPA) have been used to deal with online obscenity.

As with libel, the relatively small number of cases brought against publishers of obscene material has led many to assume that the Net cannot be regulated, but this is not the case. In the case of Regina v. Graham Waddon in 1999, for example, Waddon was charged with publishing obscene images on the Internet. Under the OPA, it is illegal to publish obscene material with a view to commercial gain, with punishment consisting of up to three years imprisonment, an unlimited fine, or both.

The fact that a large amount of pornography on the Web is free makes it difficult to apply the OPA, but Waddon was charging visitors to view his material: his defence was that these files were housed on a server in another country. An amendment in the 1994 Criminal Justice and Public Order Act, however, has clarified publication to include transmission of material, so that Waddon was found guilty of electronic transmission of such files to a server, meaning that a person could be found guilty of breaking the law in the UK even if the ISP is in a different country.

Whilst the argument in America has polarised between those advocating free speech whatever the cost and those advocating censorship whatever the cost, attempts to introduce such things as the Communications Decency Act as part of wider telecommunications bills have demonstrated some of the difficulties for the US government (or any other national government) to police the Web effectively.

Privacy

While copyright infringement has tended to concern producers and governments more than users, the problem of junk-mail, or **spam**, is one appreciated by just about everyone. Spamming occurs when an individual or company sends out a message (often anonymously) to a list of recipients. Such messages may be illegal or unsuitable for the recipient, such as pornographic links or fraudulent get-rich-quick claims; even if this is not the case, spam is usually paid for by the person downloading the message and can be a major irritation, with accounts becoming unusable because of the large number of unsolicited emails.

The problems of spamming have even caused some ISPs, such as Virgin in the UK, to sue their own customers due to the fact that spammers who send out hundreds of thousands of emails may cause the ISP's mail server to be placed on the Realtime Blackhole List, a list circulated among major ISPs that identifies domain names originating large numbers of unsolicited emails.

Protection of privacy is one area where European legislation is probably more advanced than in the US, although this is not the case with freedom of information and the 1998 Data Protection Act was criticised for its failure to address the problem of spam, emphasising as it did the responsibility of users for their own data. Nonetheless, the UK and EC governments have sought to address this issue, particularly as more and more companies collect greater amounts of information about customers online, and the individual is not entirely helpless in the face of spamming. Rather than simply deleting a message or replying to it, users can often work out where an email came from and complain to the ISP that delivered it.

7
Post-production

Once a site has been designed, it must be tested and transferred to a networked computer for others to access it, either an intranet server or one connected to the Internet. Testing is an important part of the process: dead links, loading errors, elements that do not display properly in different browsers, these and other problems if not identified will probably cause visitors to dismiss your site and not return.

Furthermore, it is extremely rare for a web site, once published, not to be updated but this is something that is not always considered when planning for a web site. As such this chapter will address issues around maintaining and developing a site as well as tools to publish it to the Web. In particular, as UNIX remains the backbone of the Web in terms of an operating system, yet is rarely encountered by desktop users familiar with Windows or MacOS, we will cover some of the intricacies of using UNIX's powerful command line interface.

Finally, once your web site is online, you need to attract visitors using search engines, news groups and even advertising. The temptation for a web producer is to assume that once a page is uploaded to a site their work is over: in most cases it will be just beginning.

Testing and managing a web site

Usefulness and usability

> 'It's easy for a computer to offer operations that don't help people.'
> (Thomas Landauer, *The Trouble with Computers*, 1995)

Landauer has written extensively about the failure of information technology to deliver on many of its promises, a problem that is not so much to do with limitations of computers than with a failure by programmers to test their applications against the expectations of users. As Landauer remarks, it is all too easy for a programmer or computer designer, who almost by definition will *love* computers, to have little time for the end-user who may be forced to employ that program because of his or her job.

The process of testing, in a sense, takes us back to the pre-production issues discussed in Chapter 2. Having made a plan for our web site (ideally in consultation with a client or supervisor) and then built the site, the next step is to test the product before releasing it into the wild. I use the term advisedly: 'releasing into the wild' is an expression frequently used to describe the process by which viruses are distributed to roam at large – and there are some sites which probably count as an information virus in terms of spreading frustration and bad practice.

Testing your site, therefore, is a feedback process: if a page does not work, or users cannot see the point of a site or find information they need, individual pages may need to be re-designed or, in extreme cases, the entire site taken back to the drawing board. As such, it is advisable to test throughout the production process to ensure that development is not too far advanced if a major glitch emerges.

When testing, two key terms from Landauer are helpful: usefulness and usability. The two terms are not synonymous, although a useful site that offers information or services that users need is likely to be less useful if it is unusable, that is visitors cannot access information. On the other hand, it is easy to create a usable site that can be navigated easily yet offers nothing worthwhile to visitors.

The most important testing that can be done – but which web producers often neglect – is to use a variety of browsers and even machines if possible. See what your page looks like in different versions of IE and Navigator, and if there is any difference on a Mac and PC. Bear in mind also that browser users can set certain effects such as text size and links to their own specifications. What effect will this have on the overall appearance of your site?

One useful way of testing your site is to run the World Wide Web Consortium HTML validator at validator.w3.org. By entering the URL of a page and selecting the type of markup language against which you wish your site to be validated, you can test for potential compatibility problems in browsers. If no errors are found on your site, you may display a successful validation sign on your site. There is also a CSS validator at jigsaw.w3.org/css-validator/.

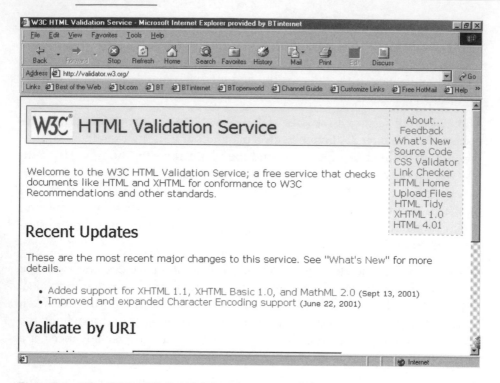

Figure 7.1   The W3C HTML validation service

Most pages written with XHTML 1.0 or HTML 4.0 will degrade fairly gracefully in older browsers, but this is not always the case when using layers: it is because of this, for example, that there are two versions of the *Web Production for Writers and Journalists* companion site, one of which is viewable in version 3.0 browsers, with the main site displaying in later browsers. If you need to test for compatibility on your own site, some useful tools include the web page purifier at www.delorie.com/web/purify.html and the backwards compatibility viewer on the same site, www.delorie.com/web/wpbcv. html. Remember to check the resources section at the back of this book and the web design resources page(www.producing.routledge.com/pages/resources_webdesign.htm) for other test sites, such as www.anybrowser.com.

Finally, test at every stage of production – what is known as formative testing. Designers may be good at testing their product at the end – summative testing – but formative testing is important to the feedback process of ongoing development.

Links and updates

More general considerations about site testing for a producer revolve around the integrity of the site structure, whether such things as links will continue to work, both internally to other pages, images and files, and to external sites. This can take some time to establish, particularly with large sites as the amorphous nature of the Web means that links to pages must be checked on a regular basis.

If a site is substantial in terms of size, this is the point where a web editor such as Dreamweaver, GoLive or FrontPage can pay dividends. These applications include management and reporting tools that can test each link, including ones to external sites if the test computer is online, and highlight dead links. Likewise, they include global search and replace tools, and the usefulness of templates in an application such as Dreamweaver really comes into its own at this point: changing an element of the template will also make changes to pages that use that template, streamlining the producer's work considerably.

As well as testing the structure of your site, ensure that you have a plan to regularly test and update the efficacy of your site's content. This will vary greatly from site to site. For example, a series of pages offering an outline of the life and work of Charles Dickens may not require updating very often if it is simply offered as the producer's opinion on that author: then again, if it is intended as a scholarly site, it may need to include updates on a monthly or quarterly basis to take into account new research. A news service, on the other hand, should have at least daily updates, and probably even hourly changes, or at least be updated as and when new stories break.

The important point is that you should have some sort of strategy where appropriate for developing your site to prevent it becoming redundant. This tends to be one of the areas that is most often overlooked, particularly for intranets and other services where a commercial benefit may not be immediately obvious yet labour and hours are required to keep the site up to date.

Publishing and managing a site

Using FTP

Files are transferred across the Web all the time using browsers and email applications, but these transfers are usually restricted to handling specific file types.

To publish files to a server so that they can be viewed requires the use of file transfer protocol (FTP) software.

FTP, unlike email, is used to transfer files to a public server rather than between individuals. The big difference between the hypertext transfer protocol and FTP is that in the latter, file transfer works both ways, uploading to, as well as downloading from, the server. FTP clients can be standalone programs such as WS_FTP for Windows or Fetch for Macs, or are incorporated into the browser with Navigator and Internet Explorer 5 and above.

FTP requires little information about the type of file that is being sent, but it does have two modes for sending files: text and binary. The former is used to send ASCII text with no changes at all and is useful for transferring HTML files to a server. Binary can send any file type at all, which can cause problems with some text files: if an HTML file or Perl script, for example, is uploaded, it may not work correctly if the file originated on a Windows or MacOS system and is being transferred to a UNIX server because the line endings are not preserved. In such cases, use text mode to transfer the files.

FTP applications

Browsers such as Internet Explorer 5 and Netscape Navigator include basic FTP capabilities that can be used to transfer files to and from a server as long as it is set up without any peculiarities (such as using a different port to the standard FTP port). To connect to an FTP server, enter the address, which usually begins with ftp:// rather than http:// in the browser; for a private directory on an ISP's server, this will usually be in the format ftp://userID:password @servername.

From the FTP server, downloading files simply consists of clicking on the selected file names. With Navigator, files can also be uploaded to a site from the menu option, File, Upload File. Using Internet Explorer 5, files can be transferred to a site by dragging and dropping them into the remote directory.

While these browsers allow users to perform basic FTP operations, the fact that they do not distinguish between binary and text files could be problematic, as is the fact that some FTP servers may use unconventional settings. In such circumstances, shareware FTP applications such as WS_FTP (www. ipswitch.com) provide a convenient graphical interface which works like Windows Explorer to drag and drop files between the local and remote hard drives.

Connection to a server is slightly different than with a web browser, providing more options as well as the address of the FTP server: this includes entering user names and passwords, as well as determining host types and the use of such features as a **firewall**. Once connection has been made, such applications display series of folders, whether the server is MacOS, Windows or UNIX based, enabling users to move files into appropriate directories.

Managing a server

Once files are placed onto a site, directories and folders must be established to contain files, permissions set for files that need to be read or executed, and any old files deleted and cleared away. If the server you are using runs Windows (or a Mac server), managing the site will be familiar from using a desktop operating system such as Windows 95 or MacOS.

Windows NT, 2000 and XP enable users to set permissions on different files down to the level of individual files as well as directories. This means that hidden files can co-exist in the same folder as publicly available web pages – for example, a section of a site that is only available to subscribers. In most cases, executable files, that is applications that must run on the server as well as being read by the browser, will be contained in a folder in which the permissions are set accordingly; it is highly unlikely, unless you have administrator privileges to the site, that you will be able to set a folder as executable. However, other files can be hidden by right-clicking on the file and changing the file properties.

While Windows is gaining ground as a web server, most servers on the Internet run the UNIX operating system to host sites. Although some ISPs only allow users to upload files to a directory on the server using FTP, some also provide access to the server to set up and maintain sites; indeed, some ISPs require files to be uploaded to a specific directory (to check for viruses, for example), and users then connect to a remote machine to move files to another directory.

Unfortunately, with the decline of DOS many users are unfamiliar with such commands and some system administrators use the rather derogatory term 'guicks' (pronounced 'gweeks') to refer to those who try to upload files to a UNIX server but have only ever encountered GUIs before. As such, the following tips are intended to help web producers get up to speed with UNIX as quickly as possible: you do not need to understand UNIX inside out to manage a web site, but you should know relevant commands and processes.

Using Telnet

Telnet is an Internet service that was extremely important in the days of bulletin boards, offering a text based application to locate and manage files: while most servers now use web pages for this type of information, Telnet remains useful for logging into remote machines and managing sites, particularly as UNIX commands can be run from the text command line. Windows 9x, NT, 2000 and XP include a Telnet application, while Mac users can download a copy of the NCSA Telnet application from archive sites such as TUCOWS (www.tucows.com).

To connect to a host computer, select Connect, Remote System and enter the name of the system to log onto (if you wish to try out Telnet, you can log onto the US Library of Congress at locis.loc.gov). The Port box should be left at Telnet in the vast majority of cases, and TermType again works in most cases with VT100 (the type of terminal that Telnet emulates). When connection is made, log on with the user name and password of your account, or guest if this is a public site.

When you have finished a session, it is advisable to type in exit at the command prompt rather than simply closing the Telnet application.

Setting permissions with UNIX

With files on the site, the final step may be to make them accessible to visitors to the site. UNIX can set permissions for who can access files down to the individual file level, which is important for security (for example, to hide certain files from general visitors but enable them to those with passwords). These permissions are set for the owner of the file (usually the person who created it), groups and other users.

Using ls –l provides a file list showing permissions, which is divided into four fields, -rwx rwx rwx, indicating the file type (usually a hyphen to represent a file, or d for a directory) and whether the owner, a specific group or other users can read (r), write to (w) or execute (x) a file: if one of these permissions is not granted, the letter is replaced by a hyphen. For example, d rwx r-x r-- indicates a directory in which the owner may read, write to and execute files as he or she wishes, a specific group may read and execute files from, and which all other users may only read.

Changing file permissions requires the chmod command, which can be used with either letters or numbers (using an octal system from 0 to 7 where 0

Some common UNIX commands

When logging into a UNIX system with Telnet, the following are some of the most common commands used to navigate around the server and set up your site.

cd   changes directory, e.g. `cd mysite/webpages`

chmod   (change mode) used to alter who can read, write or execute a file

cp   (copy) copies a file

dir   (directory) lists files in a directory

exit   terminates a Telnet session

ls   (list) lists files in directory; may be used instead of dir

mkdir   (make directory) creates a directory

mv   (move) moves a file

pwd   (print working directory) lists the current directory

rm   (remove) deletes a file

rmdir   (remove directory) removes a directory

tar   (tap archive) unpacks tar files (see below)

---

provides no permissions and 7 provides all). For example, `chmod +r myfile` activates read permissions on myfile for all users. Two commonly used numbers are `chmod 755 myfile`, which activates read and execute status for a file but only allows the owner to write to it, and `chmod 644 myfile`, setting read permissions for everyone, but allowing no one to execute the file and reserving write-to status for the owner.

Security

No computer is entirely safe. AT&T, for example, reports that on average its systems are attacked on the Internet once a day; smaller companies attract less attention, but with a server connected permanently to the Internet, security becomes a more important issue. When placing information on the Net, be proactive: find the most vulnerable spots in your system and determine the worst that could happen were it to be attacked. Data that is critical should be protected both internally and externally (and placing information on the Internet may alert you to security aspects you had not been concerned with before). As well as serious threats such as hackers and damage from viruses, anyone responsible for managing a web site should be aware of the threats from environmental dangers.

Hacking, like burglary, is a real threat on the Net, but it should not deter you from setting up a site. Most intruders, like most viruses, are relatively harmless if you are well protected and backed up. Attacks on web sites could, however, result in data being stolen or corrupted or even simply system crashes. These are rare but still occur, and so it is important to be aware of the risks and adopt a strategy to prevent problems wherever possible. Obviously, the damaging effects of system failure or data loss are most evident when running a business, but other web producers may suffer if they do not plan ahead – a student producing work for assessment, for example.

Password protection is only the first key to Internet security, but it is an obvious one: using easily recognisable passwords provides one of the easiest means to bypass any security you may have in place, and the advice given in Chapter 1 for creating a password is even more important for the web administrator than the web user. While there are various security flaws in operating systems such as Windows NT that have been routinely picked up by hackers, it still remains the case that cracking passwords remains the easiest way to break into a web site.

A good password should be easy to remember but hard to guess. A combination of random numbers, letters and cases such as pB6I9dsO is likely to keep out everyone – including you. On the other hand, keeping a note of passwords anywhere is the simplest way for them to be discovered and abused.

Two of the measures you can take to deter illegal entry are encryption and firewalls. Encryption uses two keys for every transaction: one key encrypts a file, making it unintelligible, the other decodes it. Key escrow, a method favoured by the UK and US governments but condemned by experts as less safe, places a public key in the hands of a third party which may be used by authorities to decode files. In contrast to encryption, a firewall works by sealing off a network from the Internet and only allowing authorised traffic to enter; such a firewall must be regularly audited, however, as even one weak link on a network can open up other computers.

Tips for using passwords

- **Don't use the same password for everything** A password for reading an online journal or newspaper could be much more troublesome if it's the same one you use to access online web space. Likewise, anything that requires saving your credit card number on file requires a very strong password.

- **Don't use English words or names** While passwords are usually encrypted, a typical way to try to crack them using appropriate passwords is simply to run through a large number of words.

- **Try acronyms and include numbers** A common technique for passwords is to combine acronyms of names and numbers, such as 'wadsorps99' (your password for 1999).

- **Don't write down a password** If you have to keep a record of your password, write down a hint to it instead.

Viruses are worth a special mention as they are the most common security threat to using the Internet. Again, it is not worth letting fear of viruses deter you from using the Net – most viruses are relatively harmless if important data is backed up. There are occasional disasters, but these are very rare: most incidents involve the loss of only very small amounts of data which can be a nuisance. When using the Internet, always ensure that you regularly run anti-virus software and download latest releases from the manufacturer's web site.

Promoting a site

First contact

One of the most common claims from just about any ISP attempting to sell web space and services is that one of the primary uses of the Internet is for marketing and branding a site. While this may mean that most users still have not worked out practical uses for the Net, it is also true that a web site can provide useful information about an individual, company or service in an increasingly wired world.

To be effective, a web site does not work in isolation: at the very least it should offer some form of contact for visitors who may require further, or more specific, information. In addition, an email update or posting to a relevant newsgroup will help draw attention to your web site. Emailing can be a sensitive topic. Web producers should never send out unsolicited email – spamming almost never succeeds and generates more bad customer responses than good ones. Used properly, however (and that means gaining permission before sending out emails), email can be a positive tool in conjunction with a web presence.

As well as using newsgroups and email there are other techniques for getting visitors to your site. For many users the main route into your site will be via links from other sites or, more commonly, from search engines. Setting up links may take several forms: if producers of sites of related interest are willing, you may be able to place reciprocal links in their web site in return for links from yours. Increasingly, banner advertisements are an acceptable means of communicating links.

The first stage to ensuring that a web site appears in search engines is to register it with search engines. Such engines use 'spiders' to search the Web, processing the contents of a page, but you can also speed up the process by visiting a search engine home page and most have a link to submit information about your page. To take the effort out of this, consider using www.submit-it.com: there is a charge for this, but it speeds up registration with all major search engines rather than going through the process yourself or waiting for them to find you (if they do at all). The index page of a site should include keywords and description tags so that it can be searched for more easily (see Using meta tags below).

Rather than relying on your web site to sell itself simply by virtue of personal or business information, a good trick is to include information that is likely to be picked up by search engines and will appeal to a wider range of web surfers. For example, someone who wishes to promote their kart-racing track may keep an updated list of Formula 1 race statistics, or a music distributor could provide additional background data on different groups. The time spent creating an impartial guide to a relevant topic can pay dividends if it encourages people to return to your site and spend more time there.

Using meta tags

While the important work in a web page seems to occur in between the <body> ... </body> tags where images, text, links and other elements are

Tips for site promotion

Marketing your site is an inexact science, but here are a few pointers:

- **Use your web address**   Your web address should appear every-where your phone number appears.

- **Don't rely on the Web alone**   Email can be a particularly useful tool to provide updates and reminders, as well as information targeted to requests.

- **Provide additional services**   Offer extra information around your core interest that will bring in extra visitors.

- **Keep emails you send out**   This is the best way to track infor-mation you send out and so avoid overloading visitors with irrelevant information.

- **Don't spam**   Do not use bulk email applications; most addresses included on these lists will be irrelevant and earn you a poor repu-tation. Ask for permission before you mail.

- **Register data**   If you collect information on visitors, you need to register your site to be compliant with the Data Protection Act.

- **Check the relevancy of newsgroups**   If you are promoting your web site on a newsgroup, ensure that the announcement is brief and relevant (read some sample postings before hand) unless you wish to generate complaints.

displayed, the <head> . . . </head> tags also contain other important infor-mation which can be useful for your pages when hosted on a web server.

In addition to carrying the title of a page and scripts, the head section contains information that is used by search engines when trawling through the Internet indexing various pages. The <title> . . . </title> tag itself is employed by some engines to provide relevant information, but more powerful tags are the <meta> tags, document information tags that provide important data to browsers, servers and search engines.

The most frequently used meta attributes are name and content, which are used together, for example:

```
<meta name="keywords" content="Kernow: Cornish
history and places">
```

Such a tag informs search engines that anyone interested in Cornwall should visit this site.

Though keywords are a primary use for meta tags, these also perform other functions that are important to the maintenance of a site. First of all, < meta http-equiv="refresh" content="10;url=http://www.mysite.com/mypage.htm"> will redirect compatible browsers to a new site after 10 seconds. When using such a tag, be sure to include something in the body of the page – including an alternative link – in case the browser does not work with this tag. In addition, the <meta http-equiv="expires" content="Sat. 01 Jan 2002 00:00:00"> will force a **proxy server**, that is a server housing temporary copies of a site, to reload a page from its original source once the expiry date has been reached. Use of an expiry date set in the past means your page will never be cached, which is handy if it is updated regularly.

Auditing site use

Of course, another feature of producing for the Web may be that you are hosting adverts rather than using them to promote your own site. If this is the case, you will probably need to audit advertising on your site to provide information for advertisers.

Most auditing software relies on information provided by a browser to track visits, but this may not be as accurate as it initially appears. IP addresses are usually allocated dynamically by ISPs, meaning that a visitor who logs on with the address 195.75.123.100 may be 195.75.123.101 the next day, indicating two separate visitors rather than one. Alternatively, a large corporation with a single fixed IP address leading to a firewall may be hiding hundreds of visitors as one. Cookies can be used to check whenever the browser returns to the site, but many users will disable these. Again, if a site is cached, either on the user's own computer or on a proxy server, there is no hope of tracking such use.

That said, auditing advertising remains important; each time a request is made to a server, if logging facilities have been set up by the web server it will generate an entry into a log file (a text file containing details of IP address, time, date and so on) which ISPs generally make available to commercial customers. Software such as Hit List (www.accrue.com), Webtrends (www.webtrends.com) and Analog (www.statslab.cam.ac.uk/~sret1/analog/) works by taking the log files generated by web server software and feeding it through spreadsheets to chart site usage.

Guidelines for privacy and ratings

The Internet is a conduit for a vast amount of data collected from users actively (via such things as forms) and passively (through cookies to profile visitors). As with loyalty cards, such information can be valuable to web producers in its own right, but anyone responsible for managing a web site also has to pay due attention to legislation covering data protection and privacy.

The 1984 and 1998 Data Protection Acts (which implement wider EU Data Protection Directives) attempt to provide users with a degree of protection regarding collection and use of personal data. While there is also international legislation, enforcement of data protection is always difficult with a medium such as the Web, where a complaint by a user may be made against a supplier in another jurisdiction. The fact that web sites may also be cached or mirrored adds to the difficulties of regulation, but privacy is a significant factor in e-commerce. GeoCities, for example, saw its share price fall when it was accused of mishandling data provided by users.

An attempt to implement good practice, is the inclusion of privacy state-ments, which are a response to legislation and examples of self-regulation. As well as demonstrating compliance with EU legislation, such statements are often promoted as a means of providing a competitive edge, and include details of what data is being collected, who is collecting it, how long it will be stored and the rights a consumer has with regard to access and correction/deletion.

If you are intending to produce a web site for business purposes, a privacy statement can serve as a clear indication to visitors that you are committed to good practice. Obviously, drawing attention to consumer rights is also the clearest way of inviting criticism should a site not implement such practice, so a privacy statement should be implemented in practice as well as in theory. For help in constructing a statement, visit TRUST-e (www.truste.org) or the OECD (www.oecd.org), which provide useful tools.

Finally, you may be restricting visitors from your site if it is not provided with a content rating for violence, sex and bad language. Even if there is nothing like this on your site, users who surf the Web with the Content Advisor on by default will prevent a site being viewed that is not rated. Ratings schemes are not in widespread use at present (and there are also problems with the implementation of content rating in IE 5.5), but to be on the safe side you can apply for a rating at the Internet Content Rating Association (www.icra.org). After completing a questionnaire, you are provided with the relevant HTML code to place in your pages.

Concluding remarks

Since the first edition of this book, the Internet, especially the Web, has changed a great deal. There is a great deal more scepticism today about what the Internet can offer: certainly there are fewer paper millionaires and many sites that invested without a sound business plan have failed, but this does not invalidate the Net itself. While a degree of disbelief regarding the inflated claims made for the Web during its boom period has proved to be healthy, opinion could swing too far the other way. For email, booking tickets, contacting organisations, shopping and even general entertainment the Internet has established itself in our lives in a way that means it will not quickly disappear. It will transform and develop – by becoming simpler to use and more resilient, for example – but this process of change makes it the most interesting medium to work with.

In the introduction to this book, I began by explaining that while there are many techniques and concepts that can be taught with relation to web production, this should not be at the expense of imagination and ideas. Throughout this book, you have been guided through the essential principles of web production which, as I have repeated several times, consist not only of techniques for placing text, images, links and interactive components on a page but also planning what the purpose of such a site should be. If nothing else, such forethought that goes into a web site should consist of what you wish to gain from it: web production can be an interesting and pleasurable pastime if nothing else.

At the same time, this book has concentrated on several fairly technical aspects of web design. If you choose to use a package such as Dreamweaver or GoLive, it is possible to build very competent and proficient sites without actually understanding what JavaScript is and how it works. And yet, as has been indicated several times, some understanding goes a long way, and those readers who cannot afford the latest and greatest programs can still build professional looking sites with no more than a text editor and modem connection. Many areas of web design have often been hailed as a black art, but the growth of an Internet community and the availability of help and support on the Web itself mean that this medium has the potential to be more democratic than any other. With the right skills and imagination, the gateway to Web worldwide production is open to more people than ever before.

Glossary of terms used in web production

ADSL: Asymmetric Digital Subscriber Line. Offers a much faster link than analog modems across standard copper lines.

ActiveX: a set of instructions devised by Microsoft that describes how objects interact with the browser and operating system (in contrast to Java, which only interacts with the browser).

Apache: the most popular web server software, originally developed for UNIX but available on other platforms.

applet: a program designed to be launched from within another program, typically a browser.

ARPANET: the network set up by the Advanced Research Projects Agency (ARPA) and the precursor to the Internet.

ASP: Active Server Pages. Microsoft's scripting language for creating dynamic web sites. Also used to refer to an Applications Service Provider, a company that offers software for hire across the Web.

bandwidth: the amount of information that can be transferred across an Internet connection.

bitmap: a photographic image.

cache: a temporary store of information downloaded from the Internet. Browsers look in the cache to speed up the process of downloading information.

CGI: Common Gateway Interface. A protocol enabling web pages to transfer instructions to a server.

client-server: a means of connecting computers whereby the server provides information that is accessed via the remote machine.

cookie: a text message sent from a web server to a browser and then returned by the browser to the server when the user re-visits that site. Cookies are generally used to identify users and store information between visits or generate statistics.

CSS: cascading style sheets. Enable designers to specify the appearance of a page with two specifications: CSS1 for text formatting and CSS2 for text positioning.

DHTML: or dynamic HTML. The next generation of HTML which incorporates cascading style sheets and scripting to offer more control over layout and greater interactivity.

DNS: Domain Name Services. The process by which IP addresses for registered domains are transformed into URL names (such as www.yahoo.com) and vice versa.

emoticon: emoticons, or smileys, are keyboard characters representing faces and used to denote a particular feeling, such as :-) for happiness or a joke, :-(for sadness or dislike.

error correction protocol: a technique used by modems to cancel noise generated on lines and repeat transmissions if an error is made.

FAQ: frequently asked question(s). A document designed to answer common queries and help new users.

firewall: hardware or software designed to prevent unauthorised access to a network, which scrutinises all information entering or leaving the network and rejects it if it fails certain security criteria, such as coming from an unspecified address.

FTP: file transfer protocol. One of the main systems of rules governing the transfer of information across the Internet but also used to refer to a tool for accessing Internet data.

GIF: Graphic Interchange Format. An image format that uses 'lossless' compression to make files shorter so that no information is discarded. Can only support up to 256 colours, but also can be used with transparencies or animations.

HTML: HyperText Markup Language. The series of formatting commands interpreted by the browser that determines how a page is displayed on the Web.

HTTP: HyperText Transfer Protocol. The communications protocol used to define how files link to each other and how information is transmitted to browsers.

hypertext: the presentation of documents that connect to other files or parts of the same document. Hypermedia is another term for such documents that also make use of images and multimedia elements to create links.

IAB: Internet Architecture Board. A non-governmental organisation responsible for governing protocols for communicating across the Internet.

ICANN: the Internet Corporation for Assigned Names and Numbers. Handles domain name registration and IP address allocation.

IETF: the Internet Engineering Task Force. Like the IAB, an organisation for establishing Internet standards, particularly responsible for the system of Requests for Comments (RFC).

IIS: Internet Information Server. Microsoft's web server included with Windows NT.

Internet: typically defined as a 'network of networks', the Internet is a self-governing system that connects many thousands of servers and millions of users worldwide. Computers join the Internet by subscribing to a series of standards (protocols) that define the range of services available to users.

intranet: an internal network of computers using the same software and protocols as the Internet and may connect to the Internet.

IP: Internet Protocol. A series of numbers between 0 and 255 that create a unique address for each computer connected to the Internet.

IRC: Internet Relay Chat. A system of real-time based communication whereby users can send messages to others currently online.

ISDN: Integrated Services Digital Network. A means of transmitting digital information across phone lines which tends to be more reliable than analog modems.

ISOC: The Internet Society. One of the most important Internet regulatory bodies.

ISP: Internet Service Provider. An intermediary between the Internet and the end-user, an ISP can provide IP addresses and other services to subscribers.

Java: an object-oriented programming language that has the advantage of running across multiple operating systems by using a 'virtual machine' to interpret the original code on a particular platform.

JavaScript: a scripting language, originally called LiveScript, developed by Netscape and Sun to add interactivity to web pages.

JPEG: Joint Photographic Experts Group. A means of compressing images that is 'lossy', that is extraneous information is discarded.

LAN: Local Area Network. A network of computers in a relatively small area such as an office or building, in contrast to a WAN, or wide area network such as bank networks or the Internet.

Linux: free version of UNIX incorporating software designed to run on the UNIX clone GNU (GNU's not UNIX).

MIME: Multipurpose Internet Email Extensions. Series of instructions enabling a browser to interpret different types of information.

modem: MOdulator/DEModulator. Connects a computer to the Internet across normal phone lines by translating digital signals into analog ones so they can be transmitted across copper wires and vice versa so that they will be understood as information by the computer.

MP3 or MPEG3: a highly compressed format for sound that delivers near-CD quality audio.

MPEG: Motion Pictures Expert Group. A standard of video compression commonly used on the Web.

NSF: National Science Foundation. A US organisation previously responsible for administering the Internet.

node: a network terminal, or the point where the computer is connected to the network.

packet: a unit of data sent as part of a file. Files are broken down into smaller chunks that can be sent to an address by several routes and reassembled at their destination.

PDF: Portable Document Format. Cross-platform file format devised by Adobe that enables documents to be exchanged and viewed in their original format.

peer-to-peer: in contrast to a client-server network, one that is peer-to-peer has no central server when computers are linked together.

Perl: Practical Extraction and Reporting Language. A scripting language that is commonly used on the Web to provide interactive and dynamic sites.

plug-in: software used to extend the capabilities of a browser.

PNG: Portable Network Graphics. A new graphics format combining the best elements of GIF and JPEG images.

POP: Post Office Protocol. Series of instructions governing incoming email.

port: the input for a specific Internet service, such as Web, FTP or Telnet. Port numbers are used by software to connect to that service.

PPP: *See* SLIP.

protocol: a rule or set of rules governing how computers and applications connect and communicate with each other.

proxy server: a server sitting between the user and the Internet that monitors all requests to check whether information is already stored on a local cache.

PWS: Personal Web Server developed by Microsoft for use on Windows platforms.

RFC: Request for Comments. The first stage in establishing a standard for Internet communications. RFCs are circulated to the Internet Engineering Task Force (IETF).

router: examines packets of information and sends them on to their appropriate destination.

RTSP: Real Time Streaming Protocol. A standard controlling how audio and video can be transmitted (or streamed) to multiple end-users.

scripting: a means of extending the interactive capabilities of HTML by processing a series of instructions via scripts.

SGML: Standard Generalised Markup Language. Set of formatting instructions from which HTML was developed.

Shockwave/Flash: two proprietary formats for multimedia used by Macromedia and commonly encountered on the Web.

SLIP/PPP: Serial Line Interface Protocol/Point to Point Protocol. Standards for connecting directly to the Internet from a client machine.

SMTP: Simple Mail Transfer Protocol. Series of rules governing the transmission of outgoing mail.

spam: junk or other, unsolicited email.

SVG: Scalable Vector Graphics. An open source specification for vector illustrations, similar to Flash.

TCP: Transfer Control Protocol. Along with IP, this is the standard governing communication between all computers on the Internet.

Telnet: a protocol allowing users to log into a remote computer and use it as their own.

TLD: Top Level Domain, the part of a URL that identifies its type, such as .com, .org or .net.

UNIX: operating system developed by AT&T in the 1970s and the backbone of Internet operating systems.

URL: Unique Resource Locator. The address of a page on the Web.

Usenet: newsgroup archives which are now incorporated into Internet services but which were originally text only systems of bulletin boards running alongside the early Net.

vector: used to refer to computer-generated drawings (a vector being a line between two points in a certain direction).

W3C: the World Wide Web Consortium. One of the non-governmental organisations responsible for governing standards for the Web.

WAN: Wide Area Network. A network that is distributed over a large geographical area, the Internet being the most important.

web server: a computer that distributes, or serves, web pages to client computers.

WYSIWYG: What you see is what you get. Describes editors such as Dreamweaver which lay out pages as they will appear in the browser rather than by using code tags or text that is invisible when the page is viewed.

XHTML: an extended version of HTML 4.0 that includes stricter implementation of HTML rules.

XML: eXtensible Markup Language. A means of making web documents self-describing so that they can be formatted with database-style fields.

XSL: eXtensible Style Language. The formatting language used to describe how XML documents are displayed.

HTML quick reference

The following is a compact reference to HTML tags. It is not complete, and concentrates on HTML 3.2 elements. For a more complete reference see the *Web Production for Writers and Journalists* site at www.producing.routledge. com/pages/reference.htm.

Each tag is followed by a description, as well as any attributes that may be included within the tag (for example the <font> markup may include <font size=+1 color="red">); these attributes are followed by an equals sign and an attribute. Empty tags are not followed by an end marker (such as <img>), while container tags are indicated by an ellipsis (for example <body> . . . </body>).

Tag	Description	Additional attributes
`<a> ... </a>`	Anchor marking a link	href=(url)\name=(name)\target=(name)
`<area>`	Defines an area of an image map	coords=(x, y, x, y)\href=(url)\nohref\shape=(rect, rectangle, circ, circle, poly, polygon)\target=(name)
`<b> ... </b>`	Bold style text	
`<blockquote> ... <blockquote>`	Indents text as a quote	
`<body> ... <body>`	The main content of an htm document	alink=(colour)\background=(url)\bgcolor=(background colour)\link=(colour)\text=(colour)\vlink=(colour)
` `	Line break	
`<caption> ... </caption>`	Applies a caption to a table	
`<center> ... </center>`	Centres page content	
`<dd> ... </dd>`	Definition description	
`<dir> ... </dir>`	Directory list, containing list items `<li>`	
`<dl> ... </dl>`	Definition list used for dictionary items with `<dt>` and `<dd>`	
`<dt> ... </dt>`	Definition term	
`<em> ... </em>`	Emphasis	
`<font> ... </font>`	Font attributes	size=(+ or − number)\color=(colour)
`<form> ... </form>`	Defines a form for user input	acton=(url)\method=(get, post)

Tag	Description	Additional attributes
<frame> ... </frame>	Frame definition	frameborder=(yes, no)\marginheight=\(number of pixels)\marginwidth=\(number of pixels)\name=(name, _blank, _self, _parent, _top)\noresize\scrolling=(yes, no, auto)\src=url
<frameset> ... </frameset>	Main divisions for frames on a page	rows=(pixels, per cent, number of characters)\cols=(pixels, per cent, number of characters)
<h1> ... </h1>	Level 1 heading; replace 1 with a number from 2–6 for headings for levels 2–6	
<head> ... </head>	The head of a document containing information about that document	
<hr>	Horizontal rule (line) across the page	size=(number of pixels)\width=(per cent of page)\noshade
<html> ... </html>	Defines the beginning and end of an html document	
<i> ... </i>	Italics	
<img>	Places inline image on page	src=(url)\alt=(alternative text)\align=(left, right, top, middle, bottom, texttop, absmiddle, baseline, absbottom)\border=(number of pixels)\height=(number of pixels)\hspace=(number of pixels)\vspace=(number of pixels)\width=(number of pixels)

Tag	Description	Additional attributes
`<input>`	Defines input objects on forms	align=(left, right, top, middle bottom, texttop, absmiddle, baseline, absbottom)\checked\height=(number of pixels)\maxlength=(number of pixels)\name=(name)\ size=(number of characters)\src=(url)\tupe=(text, checkbox, radio, submit, resent, hidden, image)\value= (text)\width=(number of pixels)
`<li> . . . </li>`	List item	
`<map> . . . </map>`	Client-side image map	name=(name)
`<menu> . . . </menu>`	Menu list using `<li>`	
`<noframes> . . . </noframes>`	Displays alternative content for browsers that cannot support frames	
`<ol> . . . </ol>`	Ordered list using `<li>`	start=(number)\type=(name)
`<p> . . . </p>`	Paragraph break	
`<pre> . . . </pre>`	Preformatted -ext	
`<small> . . . </small>`	Smaller font for text	
`<strong> . . . </strong>`	Strong emphasis	
`<sub> . . . </sub>`	Subscript	
`<sup> . . . </sup>`	Superscript	

Tag	Description	Additional attributes
\<table\> ... \</table\>	Defines a table	align=(left, right)\bgcolor=(background colour)\border=(number of pixels)\cellpadding=\(number of pixels)\cellspacing=(number of pixels)\rules=(none, basic, rows)
\<td\> ... \</td\>	Table data cell	align=(left, center, right)\colspan=(number)\rowspan=(number)\valign=(top, middle, bottom)
\<th\> ... \</th\>	Table header cell with bold, centred contents	align=(left, center, right)\colspan=(number)\rowspan=(number)\valign=(top, middle, bottom)
\<title\> ... \</title\>	Document title, included in document head	align=(left, center, right)\valign=(top, middle, bottom)
\<tr\> ... \</tr\>	Table row	
\<u\> ... \</u\>	Underline	
\<ul\> ... \</ul\>	Unordered list using \<li\>	type=(circle, disc, square)

Resources

The following is a list of books and web sites that may be useful for further reading and for help when building web components. For a more complete list of annotated resources, updated on a regular basis with links to new web resources, see the *Web Production for Writers and Journalists* site at www.producing.routledge.com/resources.htm.

Internet history and background

Berners-Lee, Tim, *Weaving the Web*, Orion, 1999
Cooper, Jonathan (ed.), *Liberating Cyberspace: Civil Liberties, Human Rights and the Internet*, Pluto Press, 1999
Gibson, Owen, 'Growing pains', *Media Guardian*, 3 September 2001
Jonscher, Charles, *Wired Life: Who are we in the digital age?*, Bantam Press, 1999
Naughton, John, *A Brief History of the Future: The Origins of the Internet*, Weidenfeld and Nicholson, 1999
Reid, Robert H., *Architects of the Web*, John Wiley, 1997

www.ietf.org   the Internet Engineering Task Force, responsible for Internet standards
www.isoc.org   the Internet Society, which promotes Internet development
www.w3c.org   the World Wide Web Consortium, responsible for technical standards across the Web

Culture and media

Bell, David, and Kennedy, Barbara, *The Cybercultures Reader*, Routledge, 2000
Castells, Manuel, *The Information Age: Economy, Society and Culture*, 3 vols, Blackwell, 1996–2000
Ermann, M. David, Williams, Mary B., and Shauf, Michele S., *Computers, Ethics, and Society*, Oxford University Press, 2nd edition, 1996
Featherstone, Mike, and Burrows, Roger (eds), *Cyberspace, Cyberbodies, Cyberpunk*, Sage, 1995

Fidler, Roger, *Mediamorphosis: Understanding New Media*, Pine Forge Press, 1997
Gauntlett, David (ed.), *Web.Studies*, Arnold, 2000
Hall, Jim, *Online Journalism: A Critical Primer*, Pluto Press, 2001
Herman, Andrew, and Swiss, Thomas (eds), *The World Wide Web and Contemporary Cultural Theory*, Routledge, 2000
Landauer, Thomas, *The Trouble with Computers*, MIT Press, 1995
Porter, David (ed.), *Internet Culture*, Routledge, 1996
Sardarr, Ziauddin, and Ravetz, Jerome R. (eds), *Cyberfutures: Culture and Politics on the Information Superhighways*, Pluto Press, 1996
Shields, Rob, *Cultures of Internet*, Sage, 1996
Wertheim, Margaret, *The Pearly Gates of Cyberspace: A History of Space from Dante to Cyberspace*, Virago, 1999
Whittaker, Jason, *The Internet: The Basics*, Routledge, 2002
Wolmark, Jenny (ed.), *Cybersexualities: A Reader on Feminist Theory, Cyborgs and Cyberspace*, Edinburgh University Press, 1999

www.c-i-a.com   the Computer Industry Almanac
www.ctheory.com   cultural and critical theory edited by Arthur and Marilouise Kroker
www.culturalstudies.net   cultural studies online
www.honco.net   site on online publishing and the book
www.isc.umn.edu   Internet Studies Center at the University of Minnesota
www.it.murdoch.edu.au/~cec   Centre for Electronic Commerce and Internet Studies at Murdoch University
www.newmediastudies.com   David Gauntlett's new media site
www.unesco.org/webworld/observatory   the UNESCO information society observatory
www.ycis.yale.edu   the Yale Center for Internet Studies

Web design and HTML

Adobe, *Adobe GoLive: Classroom in a Book*, Adobe Press, 2000
Carlson, Jeff, and Fleischman, Glenn, *Real World Adobe GoLive 5*, Peachpit Press, 2000
Cato, John, *User-Centred Web Design*, Addison-Wesley, 2001
Coley, Lon, *How to Use Dreamweaver and Fireworks*, Sams, 2000
Fleming, Jennifer, *Web Navigation: Designing the User Experience*, O'Reilly, 1998
Gutzman, Alexis, and Pfaffenberger, Bryan, *HTML 4 Bible*, IDG Books, 1998
Ladd, Eric, and O'Donnell, Jim, *Platinum Edition Using HTML 4, XML and Java 1.2*, Macmillan, 1998
Lopuck, Lisa, and Hampton, Sheryl, *Adobe Seminars: Web Page Design*, Adobe Press, 1997
Lowery, Joseph W., *Dreamweaver 4 Bible*, IDG Books, 2001
Macromedia, *Macromedia Dreamweaver 4 Authorised*, Macromedia, 2001
Musciano, Chuck, and Kennedy, Bill, *HTML: The Definitive Guide*, O'Reilly, 1998
Niederst, Jennifer, *Web Design in a Nutshell*, O'Reilly, 1998
Powell, Thomas A., *Web Design: The Complete Reference*, Osborne, 2000

—— HTML: *The Complete Reference*, Osborne, 3rd edition, 2000

Rees, Michael, White, Andrew, and White, Bebo, *Web Interfaces, Hypertext and Multimedia*, Prentice Hall, 2001

Rein, Lisa, *XML: A Beginner's Guide*, Osborne, 2000

Siegel, David, *Creating Killer Web Sites*, Hayden Books, 2nd edition, 1997

Spainhour, Steven, and Eckstein, Robert, *Webmaster in a Nutshell*, O'Reilly, 1999

Towers, J. Tarin, *Dreamweaver 2*, Peachpit Press, 2001

Ulrich, Laurie Ann, *Web Design: Virtual Classroom*, Osborne, 2001

Veen, Jeffrey, *Hotwired Style: Principles for Building Smart Web Sites*, Hardwired, 1997

Weinman, Lynda, and Pirouz, Raymond, *Click Here: Web Communication Design*, New Riders, 1997

hotwired.lycos.com/webmonkey   a good web developer's resource

validator.w3.org   the W3C HTML validator

vancouver-webpages.com/META/mk-metas.html   metatag generator

www.123promote.com/default.html   Web promotion tools

www.anybrowser.com   test for compatibility with any browser

www.bensplanet.com   a complete HTML reference guide

www.biginfo.net   Complete Webmaster Resource web site

web.canlink.com/helpdesk/   HTML helpdesk

www.did-it.com   tools to check your ranking in search engines

www.dsiegel.com/tips   Web Wonk: Tips for Designers and Writers

www.htmlhelp.com/tools/validator   another HTML validator

www.icra.org   the Internet Content Rating Association

www.killersites.com/core.html   tips from *Creating Killer Web sites*

www.multimap.com   collection of maps which can be linked to from a site

www.ncsa.uiuc.edu/General/Internet/WWW/HTMLPrimer.html   NCSA Beginner's Guide to HTML

www.netmechanic.com   NetMechanic monitors errors on your site with an HTML validator

www.nic.uk   registration service for UK domain names

www.pagetutor.com   lots of tutorials for HTML, JavaScript and CSS

www.skill.org.uk   the national bureau for students with disabilities; includes guidelines for web development

www.submit-it.com   automates the submitting of URLs to search engines

www.webdeveloper.com   links to other sites providing information and guidance

www.webreference.com   FAQs, articles and resources for web design

Graphics and multimedia

Cohen, Luanne, *Design Essentials*, Adobe Press, 4th edition, 2001

Cohen, Sandee, *Fireworks 2 for Windows and Macintosh*, Peachpit Press, 1999

Eigen, Brad J., and Livingston, Dan, *Essential Photoshop 6 for Web Professionals*, Prentice Hall, 2001

Green, Caro, *Flash 5 H.O.T. – Hands-on Training*, Peachpit Press, 2001

Hamlin, J. Scott, *Effective Web Animation*, Addison-Wesley, 1999

Kyle, Lynn, *Essential Flash 5 for Web Professionals*, Prentice Hall, 2000

Lowery, Joseph W., and Griffin, Dennis, *Fireworks 4 Bible*, Hungry Minds, 2001

Patterson, Jeff, and Melcher, Ryan, *Audio on the Web: The Official IUMA Guide*, Peachpit Press 1998

Persidsky, Andre, *Director 8 for Macintosh and Windows*, Peachpit Press, 2000

Sahlin, Doug, *Flash 5 Virtual Classroom*, Osborne, 2001

Ulrich, Katherine, *Flash 5*, Peachpit Press, 2000

Ulrich, Laurie Ann, *PhotoShop Web Graphics F/X and Design*, Coriolis Group, 2001

Wagstaff, Sean, and Collins, Corbin, *Animation on the Web*, Peachpit Press, 1998

Webster, Timothy, Atzberger, Paul, and Zolli, Andrew, *Web Designer's Guide To Graphics: PNT, GIF and JPEG*, Hayden Books, 1997

Weinman, Lynda, and Lentz, Jon, *Deconstructing Web Graphics 2*, New Riders, 1998

Willmore, Ben, *Adobe Photoshop 5 Studio Techniques*, Adobe Press, 1999

3bgraphics.hypermart.net   useful source of buttons, bars and backgrounds (hence the 3 'B's)

ftp.sunet.se/pub/pictures/   large collection of public domain images

webreference.com/dev/graphics   pointers to optimising graphics for the Web

www.3dcafe.com   source for 3D models and tutorials

www.abcgiant.com   another large collection of images

www.boutell.com/mapedit   a useful application for creating image maps

www.buttonmaker.com   automatic button creator for your site

www.clipart.com   free clipart for the Web

www.coolarchive.com   icons, images and audio resources arranged by type

www.cooltext.com   free logo designer

www.freegraphics.com   as the name says, a free graphics site

www.grafx-design.com/tutorials.html   tutorials for applications such as CorelDraw and PhotoShop

www.photosecrets.com/links.stock.html   links to royalty-free photos

www.real.com   contains useful tools for using and producing streaming media

www.spookyandthebandit.com   Flash goodies and tutorials here

www.webclipart.com   free clipart and tips on using images on the Web

www.widearea.co.uk/designer   discusses the basics of graphic design for the Web

CGI and dynamic HTML

Barrett, Dan, Livingstone, Dan, and Brown, Micah, *Essential JavaScript for Web Professionals*, Prentice Hall, 1999

Brown, Martin, *Perl, The Complete Reference*, Osborne, 2nd edition, 2000

Busczek, Greg, *Instant ASP Scripts*, McGraw-Hill, 1999

Dwight, Jeffrey, Erwin, Michael, and Niles, Robert, *Special Edition Using CGI*, Que, 1997

Francis, Brian, *et al.*, *Beginning Active Server Pages 2.0*, Wrox, 1998

Goodman, Danny, *Dynamic HTML: The Definitive Reference*, O'Reilly, 1998

Goodman, Danny, and Eich, Brendan, *JavaScript Bible*, IDG, 1998

Heinle, Nick, and Siegel, David, *Designing with JavaScript: Creating Dynamic Web Pages*, O'Reilly, 1997

Ivler, J. M., and Husain, Kamran, *CGI Developer's Resource: Web Programming in TCL and Perl*, Prentice Hall, 1997

Lie, Hakon, and Bos, Bert, *Cascading Style Sheets, Second Edition: Designing for the Web*, Addison-Wesley, 1999

Livingston, Dan, and Brown, Micah, *Essential CSS and DHTML for Web Professionals*, Prentice Hall, 1999

Mudry, Robert, *The DHTML Companion*, Prentice Hall, 1998

Murdock, Kelly, *JavaScript: Your Visual Blueprint for Building Dynamic Web Pages*, Hungry Minds, 2000

Schwartz, Randal, and Christiansen, Tom, *Learning Perl/TK*, O'Reilly, 1997

Teague, Jason Cranford, *DHTML and CSS for the World Wide Web*, Peachpit Press, 2001

Wall, Larry, Schwartz, Randal, and Christiansen, Tom, *Programming Perl*, O'Reilly, 2nd edition, 1996

Wyke, R. Allen, and Ting, Charlton, *Pure JavaScript*, Sams, 1999

cgi.resourceindex.com/Remotely_Hosted   remotely hosted scripts and services
cgi.resourceindex.com   collection of scripts, texts, links, etc.
ezpolls.mycomputer.com   remotely hosted polling service
www.apache.org   the home site of the popular web server, apache
www.bcentral.com   a large collection of CGI scripts and services
www.beseen.com   includes search engines, hit counters and navigation tools
www.boardhost.com   remotely hosted discussion/bulletin board
www.cgi101.com   another collection of CGI scripts
www.cutandpastescripts.com   as the name says, scripts to cut and paste into your site
www.ezboard.com   discussion/bulletin board host
www.freefind.com   a free search engine for your site
www.freeforums.com   discussion/bulletin board host
www.perl.org   the home site of this powerful scripting tool
www.pollit.com   web poll host plus other services such as guestbooks
www.responders.net   third-party form processing
www.searchengine.com   free search engine for sites with less than 500 pages
www.ultimatecounter.com   free basic counter for sites with upgrades for a fee
www.worldwidemart.com   another collection of CGI and Perl scripts
www.websiteresources.net   Microsoft's web development site

Java and ActiveX

Armstrong, Tom, Crespino, Jim, and Alumbaugh, Rob, *Active Xpert*, McGraw-Hill, 1997

Bloch, Josh, *Effective Java, Programming Language Guide*, Addison-Wesley, 2001

Eckel, Bruce, *Thinking in Java*, Prentice Hall, 2nd edition, 2001

Flanagan, David, *Java in a Nutshell*, O'Reilly, 3rd edition, 1999

Lang, Zane, *ActiveX All in One: A Web Developer's Guide*, Prentice Hall, 1997

Walsh, Aaron E., Couch, Justin, and Steinberg, Daniel H., *Java Bible*, IDG Books, 1998

www.anfyteam.com   home site for Anfy, a Java applet builder
www.devpower.com   ActiveX tools for web developers
www.freewarejava.com   lots of free applets for designers
www.gamelan.com/   a wide range of Java applets are stored here
java.sun.com/applets/index.aspl   Sun's home site for free Java applets
www.javasoft.com/applets/   information on Java and reusable examples
javaboutique.internet.com/   Java applets, articles and discussion groups
www.quickchat.org   a Java chat generator
www.active-x.com   another large collection of ActiveX tools and utilities
www.developer.com/downloads   graphics, scripts and dynamic behaviours to add
    to your site
softwaredev.earthweb.com/java   links to resources and downloads

Writing

Aitchinson, James, *Guide to Written English*, Cassell, 1996

Bagnall, Nicholas, *Newspaper Language*, Butterworth/Heinemann, 1993

Burchfield, Robert, *The New Fowler's Modern English Usage*, Clarendon, 1996

Greenbaum, Sidney, and Whitcut, Janet, *Longman Guide to English Usage*, Penguin, 1996

Hicks, Wynford, Adams, Sally, and Gilbert, Harriett, *Writing for Journalists*, Routledge, 2nd edition, 2000

Hoffman, Ann, *Research for Writers*, A&C Black, 1992

Partridge, Eric, *Usage and Abusage*, Penguin, 1973

The Oxford Dictionary for Writers and Editors, Oxford University Press, 1981

Index